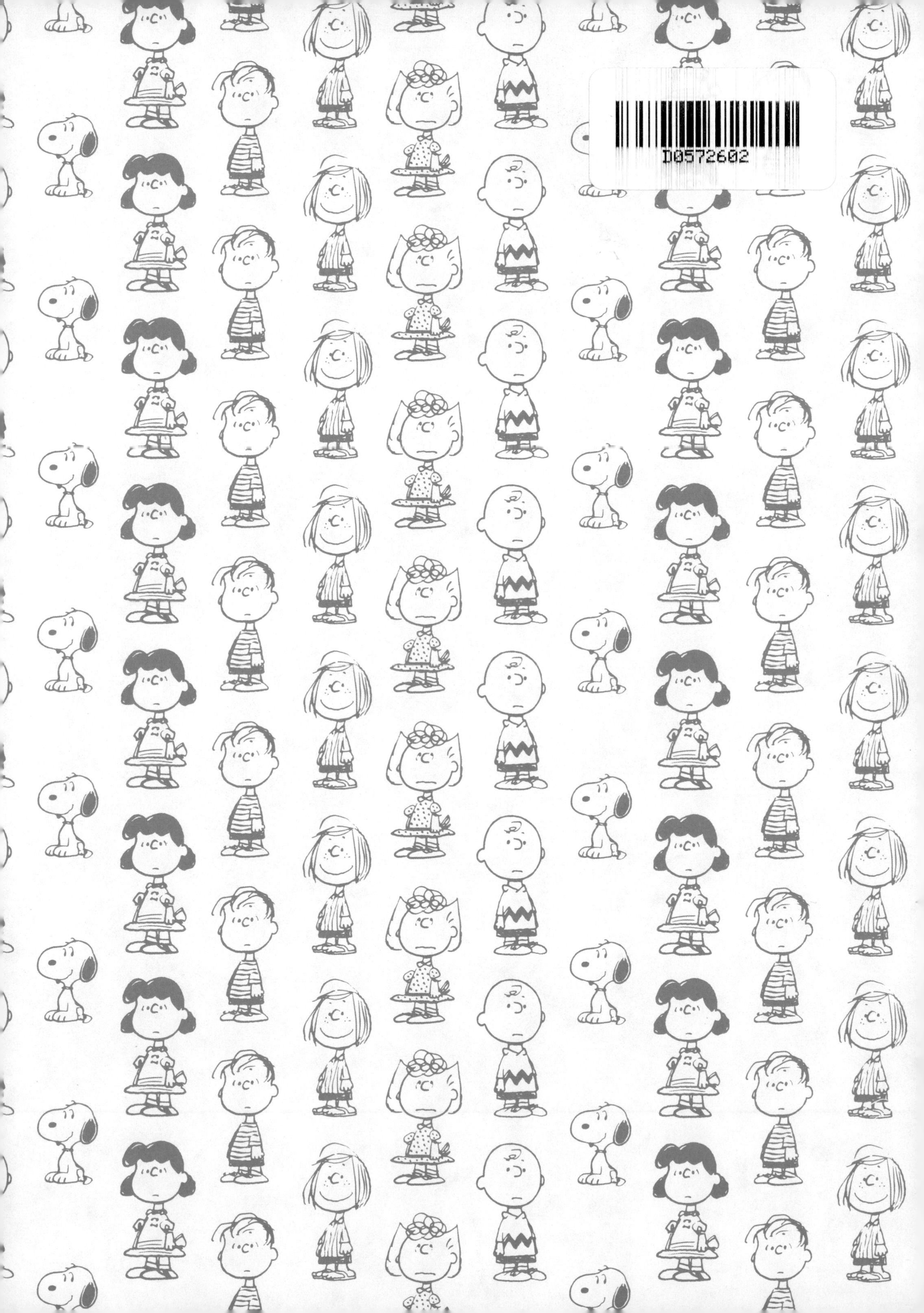

HOW THINGS WORK

Based on the Characters of Charles M. Schulz

Derrydale Books
New York • Avenel

Based on the English Language Book "CHARLIE BROWN'S
'CYCLOPEDIA—VOLUMES 6, 8, 13" © 1990 United Feature Syndicate, Inc.

This 1994 edition is published by Derrydale Books,
distributed by Random House Value Publishing, Inc.,
40 Engelhard Avenue, Avenel, New Jersey 07001

Cover designed by Bill Akunevicz Jr.
Production supervised by Roméo Enriquez

Manufactured in the United States of America

Library of Congress Cataloging-in-Publication Data
How things work / Illustrated by Charles Schulz.
        p.   cm.—(Snoopy's world)
Rev. ed. of: How machines work, Science can be super,
Electricity and magnetism, published 1992 by Funk and Wagnalls.
ISBN 0-517-11896-3
1. Machinery—Juvenile literature.   2. Science—Juvenile literature.
         [1. Machinery.   2. Science.]
I. Schulz, Charles M.   ill.   II. Title: How machines work.
III. Title: Science can be super.   IV. Title: Electricity and magnetism.
V. Series: Schulz, Charles M.   Snoopy's world.
TJ147.H69   1994
621.8—dc20
94-15103
CIP   AC

10 9 8 7 6 5 4 3 2 1

INTRODUCTION

Welcome to Snoopy's World, where, in *How Things Work*, you'll learn all about magnets, television, computers, and even video games. Have you ever wondered where escalator steps go after they disappear, or what makes cartoon characters move, or how a light bulb works? Charlie Brown, Snoopy, and the rest of the *Peanuts* gang are here to help you find the answers to these questions and many more about the way things work. Have fun!

CONTENTS

WHEELS AND AXLES: DOORKNOB, ROLLER SKATES.

CONTENTS

CONTENTS

Machines come in all sizes. They can be as big as a house or small enough to fit in the palm of your hand. They may be made of many parts, or they may be very simple, but all machines are used to do special jobs. Let's see what machines are made of and how they do their work!

MACHINES INSIDE OUT

CHAPTER 1

THE MARVELS OF MACHINES

What is a machine?

A machine is an object that makes hard work easier or slow work faster. It gives the person using it greater speed or greater force. *Force* means a push or pull. A machine is usually made up of a few connected parts. A vacuum cleaner is a machine that makes housecleaning easier. A car is a machine that lets people move much faster than they could by walking. A telephone is a machine that makes talking to someone far away possible.

What are machines made of?

Machines can be simple or complex. Simple machines are made up of only one part. Complex machines have many parts. No matter how complicated the machine, if you take it apart, you end up with a combination of simple machines. There are six types of simple machines:

1. the lever
2. the inclined plane
3. the wedge
4. the screw
5. the wheel and axle
6. the pulley

Things such as gears, cranks, and springs are based on these simple machines.

Do all machines have motors?

No. There are many machines that do not have motors. The power for doing work with many of these machines comes from people's muscles. A broom is a kind of machine that needs your muscles. If you're sweeping the floor, you need your muscles to do the pushing—though the broom makes the sweeping job easier. Scissors, a shovel, a bottle opener, and a seesaw are also examples of motorless machines that need your muscles to help do the work.

LEVERS: SEESAW, TWEEZERS CHOPSTICKS, BOTTLE OPENER, FISHING ROD AND REEL, PIANO.

WHEELS AND AXLES: DOORKNOB, ROLLER SKATES.

What machines will we meet?

Here are some examples of the machines you and your family probably use every day. So come along with the *Peanuts* gang, and they'll show you how machines work.

Machines are very old! Back in the fifteenth century, the Italian artist and inventor Leonardo da Vinci filled notebooks with drawings of simple and complicated machines!

SCREWS: FAUCET, CORKSCREW.

WEDGES: ZIPPER, SAW, KNIFE, NEEDLE, LAWN MOWER, ELECTRIC SHAVER.

SPRINGS: POGO STICK, DIVING BOARD, BOW AND ARROW, MUSIC BOX, TOASTER, STAPLER, WIND UP CLOCK, BATHROOM SCALE.

INCLINED PLANE: LOADING PLATFORM.

PULLEYS: VENETIAN BLINDS, ELEVATOR

GEARS: ALARM CLOCK, BICYCLE, ESCALATOR.

ROLLER COASTER, STEERING WHEEL.

CRANKS: EGG BEATER, HAND DRILL, PENCIL SHARPENER.

PEANUTS

CHAPTER : 2

LEAVE IT TO LEVERS

Even though levers aren't fancy or complicated, you couldn't get by without them. You use them to pry and balance things— even to play! As you look around, you'll be surprised at how much they can help you do.

LEVERS IN OUR EVERYDAY LIVES

What is a lever?

A lever (LEV-ur) is a stiff bar that turns on a point. This point is called a fulcrum (FULL-crum). The seesaw on your playground is an example of a kind of machine called a lever. When a seesaw is used by two people who weigh about the same, its fulcrum is right around the center of the bar.

With a seesaw, you can lift a person heavier than you are if the heavier person moves forward on the seesaw, closer to the fulcrum. You certainly couldn't do that without the help of a machine!

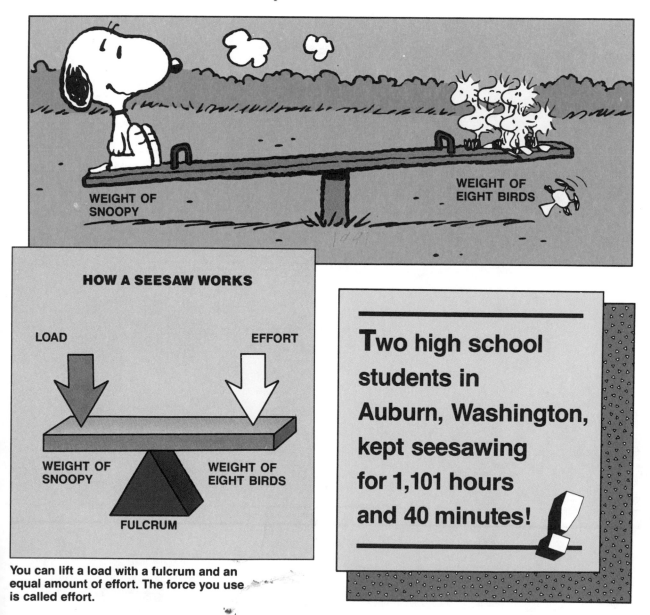

WEIGHT OF SNOOPY

WEIGHT OF EIGHT BIRDS

HOW A SEESAW WORKS

LOAD

EFFORT

WEIGHT OF SNOOPY

WEIGHT OF EIGHT BIRDS

FULCRUM

You can lift a load with a fulcrum and an equal amount of effort. The force you use is called effort.

Two high school students in Auburn, Washington, kept seesawing for 1,101 hours and 40 minutes!

13

What lever helps open bottles?

Some bottles do not have caps that are screwed on. With these bottles, it is nearly impossible to pull the cap off by hand. By using a bottle opener, another example of a lever, a bottle cap can be lifted off easily. One end of the lever is attached to the bottle. When your hand applies a small force to the other end of the lever, the cap lifts right off.

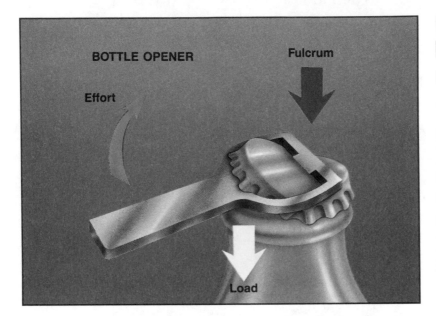

How do levers help a piano make music?

The keys of a piano are attached to levers. When Schroeder pushes a piano key, a hammer at the end of a lever strikes wires inside the piano. This action creates a sound.

What lever helps take a splinter out of your skin?

A pair of tweezers is a lever that you can use to lift a splinter out of your skin. A small movement of your fingers against the two sides of the lever creates a larger movement in the tweezers, and lifts out the splinter.

Chopsticks are helpful levers—
especially when you're hungry!

Can people use levers to eat with?

Many people around the world do just that. They eat with levers called chopsticks. Like tweezers, a small movement of the fingers against the chopsticks creates a larger movement to help pick up the food.

Chopsticks were first used in China. The name comes from the Chinese word *K'wai-tsze* (kwhy-tzoo), which means "quick ones." Made of bamboo, wood, plastic, ivory, or metal, chopsticks are now used all over the world.

Why do people use a rod and reel for fishing?

People use a rod and reel to get their bait into deep water, where the big fish are. When you fish from the edge of a lake or river, or from an ocean beach, you are far from the deep water. The fishing rod is a lever that helps you throw your fishing line farther than your arm could do alone. You also need a very long line. The reel is used to store the line neatly and keep it from getting tangled.

When the line is thrown—or cast, as fishermen say— the reel lets the line go out very far. The hand that is placed on the reel closer to the body acts as the fulcrum, the turning point, while the other hand supplies the effort.

CHAPTER 3

Have you ever tried to pull a wagon? What would happen if you had to pull it up a long flight of steps? Impossible? Well, you could try lifting the wagon, but that would be too heavy a job. No, that's not the answer at all. What you need is a ramp, one type of inclined plane that tackles tough tasks. Other variations of inclined planes—the wedge and the screw—also help to get many jobs done.

THE INCREDIBLE INCLINED PLANE

INCLINED PLANES

What is an inclined plane?

An inclined plane is a tilted, flat surface. It makes moving things between high and low places easier.

How do we use inclined planes?

An inclined plane can be used to load heavy boxes into a truck. Most people are not strong enough to lift such boxes, but placing a ten-foot plank with one end in the truck and the other end on the ground makes this task easy to do! Often this machine has little rollers on it. The rollers help the boxes slide easily up the tilted plane.

Such inclined planes, or ramps, were also used in Egypt back in 2600 B.C. to build huge pyramids and temples. These long, tilted ramps allowed workers to move very heavy stone blocks to the tops of pyramids and temples.

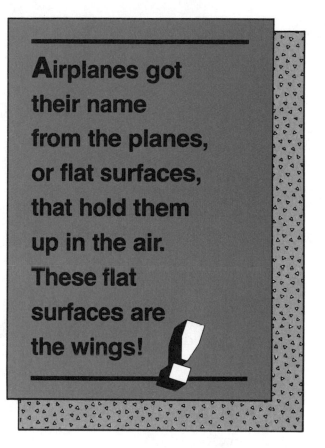

Airplanes got their name from the planes, or flat surfaces, that hold them up in the air. These flat surfaces are the wings!

WEDGES

What is a wedge?

A wedge is a special type of inclined plane. It has two or more surfaces that slope to an edge or a point. A log splitter is a kind of wedge. First the wedge is placed on the end of a log. When someone strikes the wedge with a mallet or hammer, the wedge is forced into the log. The sides of the wedge push the log apart. The wedge changes the downward force of the hammer into a sideward force that pushes the log apart. The deeper the wedge goes in, the more the two halves of the log are pushed apart. Finally, the log splits into two pieces.

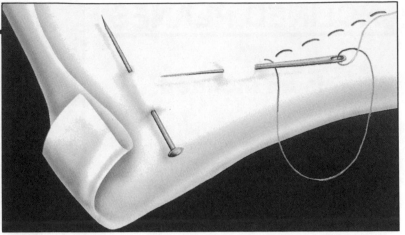

Pins and needles are two examples of wedges used on clothes.

What are some other machines that use a wedge?

Almost all machines that cut use a wedge. Axes, hatchets, and knives are sharp tools that are shaped like wedges to help them work better. Pins, needles, and nails are examples of pointed wedges. The points help the pin, needle, or nail go in easier. The material that is in the way is pushed to the side to let the pin, needle, or nail go through.

For example, a flat-ended pin would push the material ahead of it, instead of to the side. It would be very hard to make this kind of pin go through any material.

This man needs a saw with a nine-foot blade for a big task.

Some saws have teeth made of diamonds!

How does a saw work?

A saw works like hundreds of very tiny axes chopping. Each tooth on a saw blade is like a tiny, sharp ax. When you make a saw go back and forth across what you are cutting, the teeth bite off little chunks. Each little chunk is a piece of sawdust. Axes or hatchets, on the other hand, strike with a much greater force. They bite big chunks out of a piece of wood. For that reason, a saw is used for making careful, neat cuts in wood, plastic, or metal. An ax or a hatchet is used to make big, deep cuts.

Why do sharp knives cut better than dull knives?

In order to cut through something tough, such as the skin of a tomato, you need a special wedge—a knife—but its blade needs to be sharp. The reason is that sharp knife blades are thinner than dull knife blades, and sharp blades also have a rougher edge than dull ones. There are tiny teeth, so small you can see them only under a microscope, all along that rough edge of a sharp blade. If it's the blade of a steak knife, however, then it has large teeth. These teeth bite and tear at the tomato skin. Because a sharp blade is very thin, it has a very narrow area of tomato skin to push through. A dull blade is wider than a sharp blade, so it has to push through more tomato skin. A dull blade can cut only soft things, such as butter.

How do artists use wedges?

Artists who make wooden statues sometimes use a wedge called a chisel. They place the chisel against a wooden block, then bang on it with a mallet. Pieces of the wood block are cut off, and a beautiful sculpture is created.

With a simple wedge, this artist can bring a block of wood to life.

How does a lawn mower cut grass?

Lawn mowers use wedges called blades. The most popular type of lawn mower is the rotary power mower. *Rotary* means turning or spinning around. A rotary blade spins like a fan or an airplane propeller. A gasoline or electric motor supplies the energy to spin the blade. When the blade spins, it creates a wind underneath the mower. This moving air makes the blades of grass stand up straight. Then the mower chops them all off at the same height. The result is a lawn that looks smooth and even.

I HATE LAWN MOWERS!

The biggest lawn mower on record is 60 feet wide. It can mow one acre of grass in one minute!

What kind of power wedge can you find in the bathroom?

Electric shavers use wedges to cut hair, but they also need to protect the skin from getting cut. Most electric shavers have a metal screen that glides over the skin but also allows the hairs into the shaver. The screen holds the hairs in place as the cutting blades—small, sharp wedges—spin around and slice off the hairs.

ELECTRIC SHAVER

CIRCLE OF BLADES

BLADE SCREEN

There's probably a power wedge in your very own home.

ZIPPERS ARE A PAIN IN THE NECK!

What makes a zipper work?

A zipper works because of wedges! If you look at a zipper, you'll see two rows of teeth that lock together when you zip it up. A little bump on the top of each tooth fits into a little hole in the bottom of the tooth above it. The part that you pull up and down is called the slide. The slide contains wedges that magnify the small effort that you use to open or close the zipper.

Inside the slide is a Y-shaped track surrounded by three wedges. When you open the zipper, the rows of teeth run through this track and the upper wedge forces the teeth apart. When you close the zipper, two lower wedges force the teeth back together, making them mesh and lock.

On some zippers, the teeth are made of metal. Other zippers have plastic teeth, and each row of teeth looks like a long, thin spring or spiral.

SCREWS

Is a screw a machine?

Yes. Screws are really inclined planes in spiral form. When you turn a screw, its spiral threads, or ridges, turn to make the small force of your muscles into a larger force. This force helps drive a screw into wood or other objects.

How does a corkscrew work?

A corkscrew is a spiral, pointed piece of metal that is used to remove corks from bottles. One end of the corkscrew is attached to a handle. The other end—the sharp end—is placed in the center of the cork. As the handle is turned, the corkscrew is driven into the cork. Once the corkscrew is inside the cork, a strong pull will remove the cork from the neck of the bottle.

How does a faucet work?

A faucet is attached to the end of a water pipe. The faucet holds the water in the pipe until you decide to let some out.

There is a hole between the water pipe and the spigot, the part of the faucet from which water flows. Inside the faucet is a screw that drives a plug into the hole. When you don't want water to come out, you want the hole to be plugged up. When you want water, you want the hole to be open. Turning the handle in one direction causes the plug to come out of the hole. Then water flows through. Turning the handle in the other direction puts the plug back in the hole. Then water can't leave the pipe.

The ancient Romans were using water faucets about 2,000 years ago!

CHAPTER 4

Machines that roll have them . . . so do machines that spin round and round. What makes these things turn? Wheels and axles! It's a very simple idea that does some amazing things—especially when wheels are used with ropes to make pulleys.

ROUND AND ROUND, UP AND DOWN

LET'S TAKE A SPIN WITH WHEELS

How are wheels used?

Wheels help people and things move more easily. Cars and trains could not work if they didn't have wheels on which to move. Neither could bicycles, skateboards, roller skates, shopping carts, baby carriages, and many other things. Wheels sometimes connect motors to machines. In this way, motors rather than people can supply the energy to make the machines work.

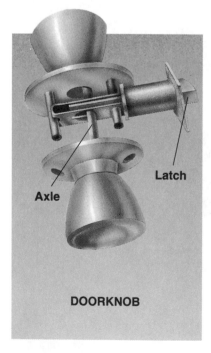

How does a doorknob work?

A doorknob is a wheel attached to a rod called an axle. The axle goes through the door. At the other end of the axle is another doorknob. When you turn one of the doorknobs, it turns the axle. The axle pushes a bar that's connected to the latch. The latch is the piece of metal that sticks out of the edge of the door. It fits into a little hole in the wall when the door is closed. The latch keeps the door from opening until you turn the knob. When you close the door, a spring makes the latch pop into the hole in the wall. The same spring also makes the doorknob turn back into place after you let go. You'll learn more about springs in chapter 5.

What makes roller skates and skateboards roll easily?

Inside the wheels of roller skates and skateboards are little steel balls called ball bearings. The ball bearings fit into grooves between the wheels and the axles. If there were no ball bearings, the wheels would rub and scrape on the axles. This kind of rubbing and scraping is called friction (FRICK-shun). It makes wheels hard to turn. If wheels are hard to turn, they can't roll fast. Ball bearings reduce friction and make wheels easy to turn. You can reduce friction even more if you squirt a drop of oil on the ball bearings. Bicycles, cars, and many other kinds of machines use ball bearings and oil or grease to make them run better.

The highest speed recorded on a skateboard is 78.37 mph in California by Roger Hickey on March 16, 1990!

How did factories make their machines run before engines and motors were developed?

They used water wheels. This meant that factories had to be built close to a fast-flowing stream or river. A water wheel was made of wood. It had paddles or buckets around the rim. Part of the wheel was always in the water. As the stream flowed, water pushed against the paddles or buckets. It made the wheel turn. The wheel was attached to an axle called a drive shaft. Drive shafts were often very large. Some were made from the whole trunk of a tall tree. The drive shaft reached from the water wheel to the inside of the factory. When the water wheel turned, it made the drive shaft run the machines. In many factories, the drive shaft was used to turn other drive shafts. In that way, many machines could run at the same time.

PULLEYS ALL AROUND US

What is a pulley?

A pulley is a wheel that has a groove in the rim to hold a rope or cord. The groove in the wheel holds a rope and keeps it from slipping off. If you hang a pulley from a high place, like a ceiling or a tree limb, you can use it to lift a heavy object easily.

With a pulley, you are not using just your muscles to lift. You are also using the weight of your body. As long as the object you are lifting weighs less than you, you can lift it with a single pulley just by attaching it to one end of the rope and pulling down on the other end.

With the help of two double pulleys, you can lift a weight that's four times heavier than you!

What makes an elevator work?

With the help of pulleys, elevators lift and lower people from one floor to another. When you step into an elevator and push the button, an electric motor starts up. The motor is in a room at the top of the building. The motor pulls a set of cables that lifts the box in which you are riding. This box is called the elevator car. Each cable is a rope made of wires twisted or woven together. The cables run over pulleys attached to the motor. The end of the cables not attached to the car go down the elevator shaft to a counterweight. A counterweight is a weight that balances the car. When the car goes up, the counterweight goes down. When the car goes down, the counterweight goes up. An elevator has an automatic brake that stops the car if it begins to fall.

How do venetian blinds open and close?

Inside the venetian blinds, there's a pulley that makes them open and close. When you pull on a cord, it sets off a chain of events. The cord turns a pulley. The pulley turns a screw. The screw turns a gear. (You'll learn more about gears in chapter 5.) The turning gear then changes the slant of the top strip, or slat. This changes the slant of all the slats in the blind. As the slats move into a horizontal position, more light can come in. Horizontal means that the flat part of the slat faces the ground.

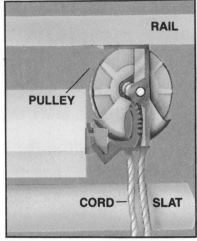

Behind every venetian blind is the magic of a pulley.

How do venetian blinds go up and down?

They go up and down with a cord and pulleys. To make the blinds go up or down, you pull the cord down or let it go up. This cord is different from the one that opens or closes blinds. It's threaded through a few pulleys in a heavy rail above the top slat. It also passes down through holes in all the slats to the bottom bar. When you pull down on the cord, the bottom bar is pulled up. Along with the bottom bar, up go the slats.

PULLEYS ARE HANDY, BUT IT'S MORE FUN TO PEEK THROUGH THE SLATS.

CHAPTER 5

So you want to pedal your bike, sharpen your pencil, or take a dive into the swimming pool? Well, then, you'll need gears, cranks, and springs. You'll find these helpful machines just about everywhere!

TAKE ACTION WITH GEARS, CRANKS, AND SPRINGS

GET INTO GEAR!

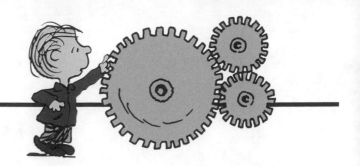

What is a gear?

Gears are wheels with teeth. These teeth can be curved or straight. Gears do nothing alone—but they work well together! Their teeth mesh with the teeth of other gears of many shapes and sizes, like puzzle parts. Many gears working together can help you do incredible tasks!

How do the gears on a one-speed bicycle work?

A one-speed bike has two gears called sprockets. One sprocket is attached to the pedals. The other is attached to the rear wheel. A chain goes around the two sprockets. When you pedal, you turn the pedal sprocket. This pushes the chain, which turns the rear-wheel sprocket. That turns the wheel to make the bike go.

BIKE GEARS

Why do some bicycles have ten speeds?

If a bicycle has ten speeds, the rider can make the bike go fast without pedaling fast. Ten gears also help the rider pedal up a hill without straining too hard. When you ride a one-speed bike, some hills are too hard to ride up. You have to get off and push the bike. If you want to go fast on a one-speed bike, you have to pedal very, very fast, and you soon get tired. Three-speed bicycles are better for climbing hills or going fast because they have more gears than one-speed bicycles. More gears mean more possible speeds. Ten-speed bikes are even better.

How do the gears on a ten-speed bicycle work?

A ten-speed bike has seven sprockets. Two are attached to the pedals, and five are attached to the rear wheel. Each sprocket is a different size. The chain is always looped around one of the pedal sprockets and one of the rear-wheel sprockets. The bike has controls that let you move the chain from one sprocket to another. By doing this, you can get more speed or more forward force—but not both at the same time.

If you wanted to go fast on flat ground, you would put your chain around the largest pedal sprocket and the smallest rear-wheel sprocket. This combination would give you the most speed but the least force. You don't need much force to move on flat ground.

If you wanted to go up a hill without pedaling hard, you would need a lot of forward force. So you would put your chain around the smallest pedal sprocket and the largest rear-wheel sprocket. This combination would give you the most forward force but the least speed. You would go up the hill easily but slowly. Ten combinations of rear-wheel and pedal sprockets are possible. That is why the bicycle is called a ten-speed bike.

A TEN-SPEED!!
YOU CAN'T EVEN
REACH THE PEDALS

How do clocks work?

You'll find gears inside a mechanical clock. The hands are moved by a gear that turns once every hour. There is another gear behind the knob you use to set the alarm. On it is a special trigger bump. At the set time, a hole in the gear of the hour hand meets up with this bump. When the bump goes into the hole, the hour-hand gear moves closer to the alarm gear. This movement causes a hook holding a hammer to be pushed out of place. The hammer is released and it hits a bell. *Rrrrrrrriiiiiiiinnngg!* When you shut off the alarm, the hook holds the hammer still once again.

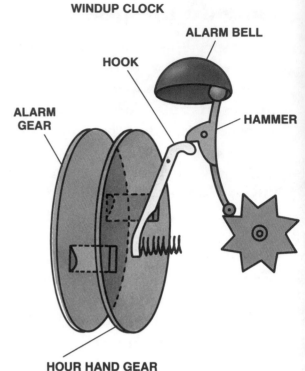

WINDUP CLOCK

ALARM BELL

HOOK

ALARM GEAR

HAMMER

HOUR HAND GEAR

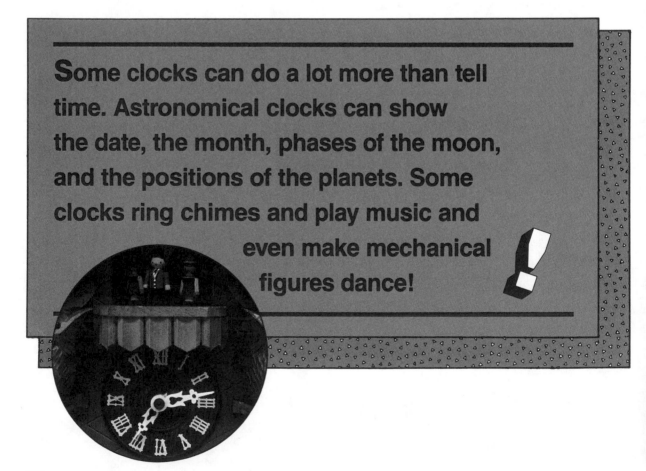

Some clocks can do a lot more than tell time. Astronomical clocks can show the date, the month, phases of the moon, and the positions of the planets. Some clocks ring chimes and play music and even make mechanical figures dance!

How do gears make an escalator work?

An escalator gets its power from a strong electric motor. The motor is connected to a gear that moves a chain. This chain is just like the chain that connects the pedals and rear wheels of a bicycle, but it's much bigger. The chain is connected to the escalator's steps. The motor turns the gear, and the gear moves the chain. The moving chain makes the steps move along tracks. Underneath, where you can't see, each step has wheels that run along tracks. These tracks are very much like the tracks that trains run on.

When a step reaches the bottom of the escalator, it goes underneath, then comes out again at the other end, at the top of the stairs. All the steps are hooked together like the links of a chain.

Escalators can move at either 90 or 120 feet per minute. Most stores use the slower speed to give customers time to look at merchandise. Escalators used in airports or subway stations usually run at the faster speed because people are in a hurry to go to exciting new places, to go to work, or to get home.

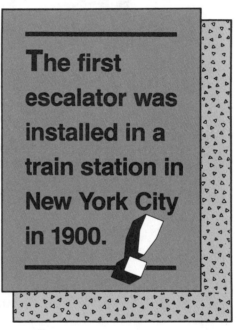

The first escalator was installed in a train station in New York City in 1900.

HAND RAIL

BELT

STEPS

GEAR

CHAIN

RETURNING STEPS

What makes a roller coaster go?

To get started, the roller coaster cars hook onto a chain. It pulls them to the top of the first hill. The chain can pull the cars because gears connect it to a motor on the ground. When the cars get to the top of the first hill, the hooks let go. Then gravity takes over. The cars roll down. They go faster and faster until they reach the bottom. As the cars go up the next hill, they slow down. The same force of gravity that makes the cars go faster when they are coasting down makes them slow down when they are coasting up. Each hill that the cars go up is a little lower than the hill that the cars just rolled down. This is because gravity and friction do not let the cars roll to a place as high as the hill they just came from.

How does a steering wheel make a car turn?

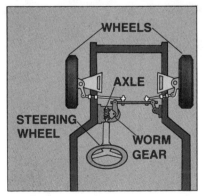

A steering wheel is connected to a long metal bar, like an axle. It extends down into a metal gearbox in the front of the car. When you turn the steering wheel, you make the bar turn a gear. In many cars this gear is a worm gear. A worm gear is a shaft or pole that is threaded—has special ridges—like a screw. This threaded part connects with one or more gears to change the speed, force, and direction of the rotation.

The worm gear turns another gear, which is connected to a lever. The lever is connected to two rods. One rod is attached to the left front wheel, and the other is attached to the right front wheel. When you turn the steering wheel, the gears move the lever. The rods attached to the lever make the car's front wheels turn left or right.

CRANK IT UP!

Is a crank a grouchy person?

Yes, but the word *crank* has another meaning, too. On a machine, a crank is a bar or handle that you turn in order to make a wheel or axle turn. When the wheel or axle turns, the machine works. The pedals on a bicycle are cranks. When you pedal, the wheels turn and the bike moves. The handle you turn to make a car window go up and down also is a crank.

Why is an eggbeater better than a fork for whipping cream?

You can whip cream faster with an eggbeater than you can with a fork because an eggbeater has a crank. When you turn the crank, it turns a large gear. This gear then pushes two smaller gears that are attached to the two beaters. As these three gears turn, their teeth hook into one another and then unhook again. Each time the big gear goes around once, the little gears go around a few times—and so do the beaters. This means the little gears are turning faster than the big gear, so the beaters are spinning faster than you are turning the crank. An eggbeater helps you by changing slow cranking into fast beating.

What machine looks like an eggbeater?

A hand drill looks like an eggbeater. It has a crank and gears like an eggbeater, but instead of beaters, it has a chuck and a bit. The bit is the part of the drill that actually makes the holes. Some bits look like wood screws. The chuck holds the bit in place.

When someone wants to drill a hole in wood, metal, or plastic, here is what must be done: The person drilling holds the bit against the proper spot and turns the handle. The crank turns the gears. The gears turn the chuck and the bit, creating the hole.

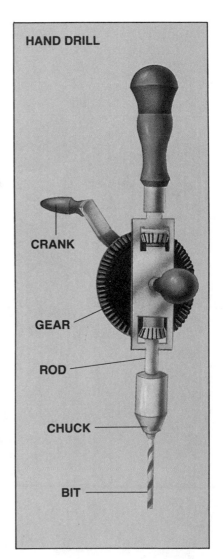

HAND DRILL

CRANK

GEAR

ROD

CHUCK

BIT

35

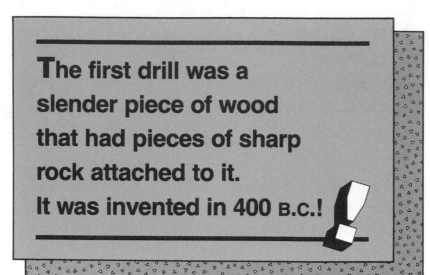

The first drill was a slender piece of wood that had pieces of sharp rock attached to it. It was invented in 400 B.C.!

How does a pencil sharpener sharpen pencils?

Inside a hand-cranked sharpener, there are two metal rollers side by side. Sharp ridges, almost like knife blades, stick out from the rollers. These ridges are for shaving little pieces of wood off a pencil. The pencil fits into a space between the two rollers. The space is wide at one end. It comes to a point at the other end. When you turn the crank, the rollers spin. They shave your pencil into the same shape as the space between the two rollers. An electric pencil sharpener has a motor instead of a hand crank.

The lead inside a pencil isn't really made of lead. It's mostly a soft, black mineral called graphite!

Spring into action!

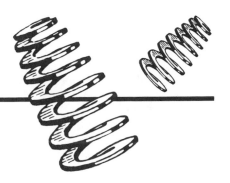

How do springs work?

Springs are used in three main ways in machines. Springs can be used to keep things in their original positions. If an object is pushed down, the spring will help pop it back into its original place. Some beds have mattresses with springs in them. The springs sink a little when you get into bed. After you get up in the morning, the springs return the mattress to its original height.

Another way springs are used is to store energy. If you push down on a spring, it stores the energy that was used to push it down. As the spring goes back to its original shape, it releases the energy, which can do work. This type of spring can be found in a clock.

Springs are also used to measure force. If you pull on a spring, the amount that the spring moves is directly related to the force that you applied. This is why springs can be used inside scales to help weigh things.

What makes springs bouncy?

Springs are bouncy because they have elasticity (ee-lass-TISS-ih-tee). This means you can stretch them or bend them or squeeze them, and they will quickly go back to their original shape when you let go. Rubber bands also have elasticity. That's why people often call them elastic bands.

How does a pogo stick help people jump high?

A pogo stick has a spring inside it. A spring, or any elastic thing, can store energy. When you jump down on a pogo stick, you use energy to squeeze the spring. The spring stores the energy for just a moment, until you start to jump up. Then the energy in the spring is let out. It gives you an extra boost and helps you to go higher.

In 1985, Guy Stewart kept jumping on a pogo stick until he had made 130,077 jumps!

HAVE YOU BEEN STORING ENERGY IN YOUR POGO STICK?

Is a diving board a machine?

Yes, a diving board is really a spring. Springs aren't always shaped like a curly piece of wire. Springs can be flat, and they can even be made of wood. Anything that bends without breaking and then snaps back to its original position is a spring. Divers like a springy diving board because it helps them to jump high. When divers jump high, they have time to do fancy tricks in the air before they plunge into the water.

How do a bow and arrow work?

The bow is a spring. When you pull back the string, you bend the bow and put energy into it. When you let go of the string, the energy is let out of the bow very suddenly. It gives the arrow a strong, fast push.

An arrow is not very heavy. You could throw it with your hand, as if it were a spear, but it wouldn't go very far. This is because your hand can't push the arrow as fast as the bow can. The faster you push the arrow, the farther it will travel. Some very strong bows can shoot an arrow half a mile!

What makes a music box play when you wind it up?

A music box is powered by a spring that works like a motor. This kind of spring is a flat piece of metal rolled up like a spool of ribbon. When you wind up the spring, you are rolling it tight. That also puts energy into it. When the spring is released, the energy stored in it makes it unwind and turn around in a circle. When the spring turns around, it turns a gear. This gear turns a second gear, which is attached to a roller. The roller has little spikes sticking out of it. When the roller turns, the spikes push aside thin pieces of metal called reeds. The reeds twang like strings of a guitar, and you hear music.

The highest price paid at an auction for a music box was $37,620 in 1985. It was a Swiss-made box that originally was made for a prince in 1901!

40

Why does a windup clock or watch tick?

A clock or watch ticks because it keeps stopping and starting again. A windup clock or watch is powered by the same kind of spring that runs a music box. The spring turns gears, which make the hands go around. If the gears kept turning without ever stopping, the energy in the spring would escape very fast. The hands would whirl around too quickly. So something called an escapement (eh-SCAPE-ment) was invented to keep the hands of the clock from spinning around too fast.

Here's how it works. Inside the clock is a tiny lever. It is shaped like a Y at one end, with two hooks at the tips. The lever flips back and forth like a seesaw going up and down. Each time the lever flips, one of the hooks catches a tooth on one of the clock's gears, stopping the hands for a fraction of a second. Then the lever flips again, letting the gears turn one tooth's worth until the other hook catches and stops everything again. Stop and go, stop and go. *Tick, tick, tick, tick.* Each tick is the sound of a hook letting go of a gear tooth.

You can see a watch stopping and starting. Just keep your eye on the jerky motion of the second hand!

How does a toaster know when to pop up?

Inside a toaster is a timer, which is just like a clock. When you push the knob down to start the toaster, you are also winding up the timer. The timer goes *ticka-ticka-tick* while it's unwinding. When the timer is all unwound, it releases a spring that makes your toast pop up. If you set your toaster for light toast, the timer will run fast. If you choose dark toast, the timer will run slowly.

Today, many toasters use a new type of timer called thermal sensors. When these sensors feel the toaster's heat, they pop up your toast.

How does a stapler work?

A stapler is like a big pair of tweezers, but something special happens when you push the two ends together. Inside a stapler is a row of staples, and pushing down on the stapler drives a bar against the front staple, forcing it through the papers. The ends of the staple are bent back when they hit a metal plate underneath. When you let go, a spring opens the stapler back up. Inside, another spring pushes against the row of staples, moving the next staple under the bar, ready to use again.

How does a bathroom scale work?

A bathroom scale uses a spring to measure weight. When you stand on the scale, you cause a bar to pull down on the spring. The spring stretches. The heavier you are, the more it stretches. As the spring stretches, a piece of metal swings down and pushes a second bar. This bar is long and flat and has gear teeth along one edge. It turns a small gear. The small gear turns an axle, which turns a wheel. The wheel has numbers printed on it. These numbers show through the window in the top of the scale. When the wheel stops turning, you see a number under the pointer. This is how much you weigh.

Do all scales have springs?

No. Doctors and nurses weigh people on scales that have no springs. This kind of scale uses a lever to measure weight. The lever works like a seesaw. When you step on the scale, the weight of your body pulls down one side of the lever. The other side of the lever has metal weights. These can slide along bars that have numbers. The doctor or nurse moves the metal weights back and forth along the bars until the lever balances. If a person weighs 82 pounds, for example, the lever will balance when the big weight is on 50 and the small weight is on 32 (50 + 32 = 82). Doctors and nurses prefer this kind of scale because it is more exact than a bathroom scale.

I GAINED 2 POUNDS?

CHAPTER 6

Machines have changed our lives in many ways. Without them, we wouldn't have all the terrific books we read and all the wonderful clothes we wear today. Who invented them? Charlie Brown is here to help you meet some famous inventors of machines.

WHO INVENTED...?

SEWING MACHINE

MACHINES AND THE WRITTEN WORD

Johannes Gutenberg invented the printing press more than 500 years ago.

Who invented the printing press?

A German man named Johannes Gutenberg (yo-HAHN-us GOOT-un-berg) invented the printing press around 1450. Before that, Chinese and Europeans carved wooden blocks and pressed them against paper or copied the books by hand. Gutenberg's press used a separate piece of metal type for each letter. The type could be moved around to form words. Once the type was put in order, the printer put ink on it. Then he placed a piece of paper over the type and turned a giant screw. This pressed a big wooden block against the paper, and the ink left its mark.

How are modern books printed?

Computers, photography, and even laser beams are used to prepare the type for press. For printing large numbers of newspapers, magazines, and books quickly, very big automatic presses are used. Modern presses print thousands of newspapers in an hour.

Some modern printing presses are bigger than a bus and use whole truckloads of paper and ink!

45

Who invented the typewriter?

An American named Christopher Scholes invented the typewriter in 1867. He sold his invention to the Remington company, which made hundreds of early typewriters.

Remington typewriter in 1902

How does a typewriter work?

A typewriter has little pieces of metal in the shape of letters, numbers, and other symbols. The pieces, called type, are attached to levers called type bars. The buttons that you tap with your fingers are called keys. The keys are connected to the type bars by rods and levers. When you push down on a key, a bar pops up. The type hits the inky ribbon and marks the paper.

Most electric typewriters work in a similar way, but the electric motor makes everything work much more quickly and easily. Instead of levers, a central ball or wheel containing all the letters strikes the ribbon.

You can probably write about 20 words a minute. The fastest typist can type 150 to 200 words a minute!

MACHINES AND THE CLOTHES WE WEAR

Who invented the cotton gin?

In 1793, Eli Whitney invented a machine that took the seeds out of cotton. It was called a cotton gin. Before Whitney's invention, people had to take out the seeds by hand. This was very slow work. It limited the amount of cotton a farmer could grow and sell.

Whitney's cotton gin used a hand crank to turn two rollers. One roller had metal claws to pull the cotton off the seeds. The other roller had bristles to brush the cotton off the claws. Once this was done, the fluffy white fibers could be gathered up and made into thread, yarn, and cloth.

Modern cotton gins are larger and faster than Eli Whitney's, but they are based on his idea.

Eli Whitney in his workshop building the first cotton gin.

Did Eli Whitney invent anything else besides the cotton gin?

Yes. Eli Whitney invented a way of making things quickly. It is called mass production.

In the 1700s and before, people built machines one at a time. This process was slow, and no two machines came out exactly alike. Whitney changed all that. He started mass production of guns called muskets. He made batches of musket parts at once. He made all the barrels exactly alike. He made all the triggers exactly alike, and so on. In this way, a factory worker could take one of each part and put together a musket. Other workers could each specialize in making one kind of part. Whitney showed his idea to the United States government in 1798. He was hired to make 10,000 muskets for the army. Modern factories still use Whitney's idea to make almost anything you can think of.

Who invented the sewing machine?

Everyone thinks of the American Elias Howe as the inventor of the sewing machine. Howe's design in 1846 was the most successful, but it was not the first. A sewing machine was invented as long ago as 1790 by Thomas Saint of England. His machine was made for sewing leather. A tool called an awl pushed holes in the leather. A needle stitched through the holes.

ELIAS HOWE

How does a sewing machine make stitches?

When you sew by hand, you use one thread. However, when you sew with a sewing machine, you use two threads. One thread comes down from the top of the machine and goes through the eye of the needle. The other thread is in the bottom of the machine. It is wound on a small spool called a bobbin. The needle pushes the top thread down through the cloth. When the needle is down as far as it can go, a hook in the bottom of the machine catches the top thread. The hook wraps the top thread around the bottom thread, and makes a stitch. When the needle goes back up, it pulls the top thread and makes the stitch tight.

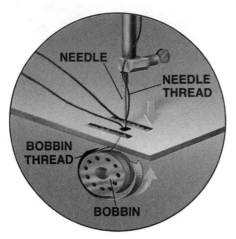

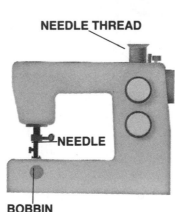

When was the zipper invented?

Whitcomb L. Judson of Chicago invented the first zipper in 1891, but the early zippers weren't very reliable. Often they jammed so that they couldn't be opened or closed. Sometimes they suddenly popped open all by themselves. It was safer to wear clothes with buttons.

Then in 1913 Gideon Sundback of Sweden invented an improved zipper that was reliable. Still, zippers weren't really around much until the late 1920s. That's when the leading fashion designers began to use them.

CHAPTER 7

Welcome to the future! Computers, video games, robots—people of long ago would never have believed the magical machines of today! The age of electronic machines has arrived.

THE FUTURE IS HERE

THE ELECTRONIC AGE: COMPUTERS AND DIGITAL DISPLAYS

What is a computer?

A computer is a machine that can remember and sometimes even learn. It has special materials in it called semiconductors (seh-mee-kon-DUCK-tours) that help it decide what to do.

Computers can be given instructions on how to do hard things, and then the computer remembers the instructions when it needs them. These instructions are called programs. People who make instructions for computers are called computer programmers. Once a computer is programmed, it can perform millions of instructions in less than a second!

LARGE COMPUTER   **PERSONAL COMPUTER**

How do we use computers?

Some computers tell other machines and people what to do. Spacecraft have computers that tell the rockets how to work and the astronauts where to steer. Other computers can play games, teach you things, and help you write or draw. They can even speak to you and play music. You can tell a computer what you want it to do by typing on a keyboard or by using a pointer called a "mouse." The computer responds to you by writing on a screen called a monitor, or by printing on paper. A computer can be bigger than a car or small enough to fit into your pocket!

50

On some computers, you don't even have to type on the keyboard. You can just talk to the computer, and it understands what you want it to do!

Does a computer ever forget what you tell it?

Actually, most computers will forget what you tell them if you turn them off. So, when you turn them back on, you have to give them a new program with instructions on what to do. Some programs are kept on floppy disks, which are very thin and flat. The floppy disk is put inside a slot in the computer called a disk drive. The computer then gets the instructions from the disk and knows what to do. Some computers also have disks built right into them that can hold many programs. These are called hard disks.

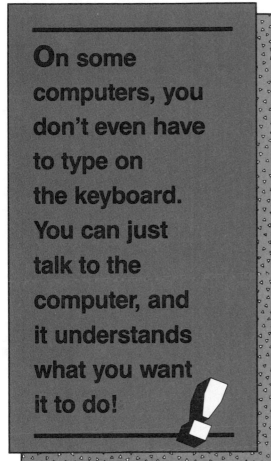

What is a word processor?

Word processors are computers that work something like typewriters. You type on them the same way you do on a typewriter, but your words appear on a screen instead of on paper.

You can tell the computer to erase or add words anywhere. You can even move sentences and whole paragraphs around. This way you can change what you wrote without having to start over! When you are all done, you can tell the computer to print what you've written, and it comes out perfect.

How do computer printers work?

Some computer printers work much like typewriters, and others use lasers to print both letters and pictures. The most common printer is called a dot-matrix (daht-MAY-tricks) printer, which works like a typewriter. This prints lots of tiny dots into patterns that look like letters. Instead of a piece of metal pressing against an inky ribbon, as in a typewriter, tiny pins on a dot-matrix printer press the ribbon onto the paper. If you look closely at printing from a dot-matrix printer, you can see all the dots.

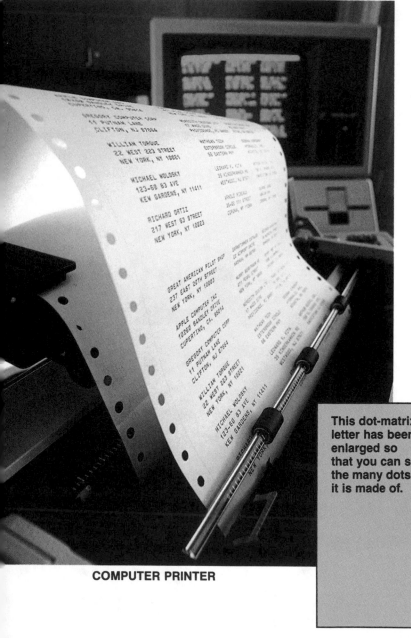

COMPUTER PRINTER

This dot-matrix letter has been enlarged so that you can see the many dots it is made of.

52

IF WE WATCH TV ALL THE TIME, WE WON'T HAVE TO LEARN TO READ...

IF WE USE WORD PROCESSORS AND CALCULATORS, WE WON'T HAVE TO LEARN TO WRITE OR DO MATH...

5-30

PRETTY SOON WE WON'T HAVE TO KNOW ANYTHING

THAT'S WHEN I'LL FIT IN!

The earliest electronic computer was called the Colossus. It was used in 1943 in England during World War II to break Germany's secret codes!

Is a calculator a computer?

Calculators are very simple computers. They know how to add, subtract, multiply, and divide numbers. Calculators can also help you figure out more difficult math problems.

HALF PAST A FRECKLE.

Is a digital watch a computer?

No. Digital watches use many of the same ideas as computers, but they are much simpler. Instead of the springs and gears in mechanical watches, digital watches have semiconductors in them that act as timers. Digital watches light up a display of numbers rather than use hands to show the time.

53

Video Games

How does a video game work?

Video games have a computer inside them that knows all the rules and moves of the game. When you play, you tell the computer what you want to do by typing on a keyboard or by moving special knobs or levers. The computer shows you what is happening in the game by the images on its screen and by making lots of beeps and noises.

COCKPIT OF A FLIGHT SIMULATOR

FLIGHT SIMULATORS MAKE ME AIRSICK!

How do airplane pilots use video games?

Pilots use fancy video games to learn how to fly. These are called flight simulators. A flight simulator draws pictures on its screen that look like what pilots might see outside a plane's cockpit window. This allows pilots to pretend that they are flying a real plane. When a beginning pilot loses control over his "plane," the computer shows a picture of a crash, but nobody gets hurt!

ROBOTS

How do robots know what to do?

Robots are machines that can move around by themselves. Most robots are controlled by computers. Robots are helpful because they can do jobs that are tiring. They don't have to stop and rest as people do, and they can move very accurately or do a job many times in exactly the same way. Robots are also good for jobs that are too dangerous for people—like defusing bombs or working with harmful chemicals.

Robots were used in the 1700s to entertain wealthy people!

Robots come in all shapes and sizes.

Do robots look like mechanical people?

No, most robots don't look very much like people. Our bodies are so complex that we can't even come close to making a machine that does as many different things as a person. Instead, robots are made for very specific jobs and can do just a few things. The way a robot looks depends on what it has to do. Robots in factories often look like mechanical arms that are bolted to the floor. The arms can swing around to build things. Other robots have wheels so they can move on their own. These types of robots can help deliver mail in large office buildings.

55

DID YOU KNOW...?

● You've just invented a super-duper marble-polishing machine. How can you protect your new invention? Get a patent! When inventors patent their machines, they get exclusive rights from their government to make and sell the machines. This means that no one is allowed to copy their machines, and no one else is allowed to make money from their ideas. In the United States, a patent lasts for 17 years. After that time anyone can copy and sell the inventor's original idea.

● A parking meter is really a type of clock. When you put a coin in the slot, the coin drops into a system of levers. The levers figure out how big the coin is. When you turn the knob, a pointer comes into the window to show you how much time you have paid for.

By turning the knob, you also wind the clock inside the meter. If you listen closely, you may be able to hear it ticking. The clock slowly moves the pointer backward to let you know how much time you have left. When your time runs out, a flag pops up in the window of the meter.

● Virtual reality is a new 3-D computer that makes you feel as if you are really there! Someday, you'll put on a helmet and "enter" a video game!

BEING A WORLD FAMOUS ATTORNEY, YOU MUST KNOW HOW TO APPLY FOR A PATENT.

● *A-choo!* Because he was sick of sneezing, Melville R. Bissell came up with a great invention!

Bissell owned a china shop in Grand Rapids, Michigan. All the china that arrived at his shop came packed in dusty straw, and Bissell was allergic to straw dust. After he unpacked a shipment of china, he needed to get the dust out of his shop. Otherwise, his allergy would bother him. This was back around 1876, before vacuum cleaners were invented. So Bissell invented a sweeper with a built-in dustpan. When he used it, the dust went into the pan, not into the air. Bissell's sweepers soon became popular in many parts of the world.

● You are almost finished drawing a picture of a tree when you notice a pencil smudge. Thanks to Hyman L. Lipman, you can use the end of your pencil to erase that smudge!

Back in the 1850s, pencils and erasers had already been invented, but Lipman was the first to think of fastening them together. In 1858, Lipman took out a patent on his idea. Today, people don't have to hunt around for an eraser each time they make a mistake.

57

Can you hear the sound of a pin dropping? Probably not. There are all sorts of sounds you *can* hear, though, from the sweet, chirping sound of a tiny bird's song to the big, crashing sound of a brass marching band. How are sounds made, and how do we hear them? Let's find out.

LISTEN TO THE SOUNDS

CHAPTER 8

SOUND AND HOW WE HEAR

What is sound?

Sound is what you hear when something vibrates—moves back and forth quickly. If you stretch a rubber band and twang it, you can see the vibrations that cause the sound. Or try it with a guitar. You can see the vibrations when you pluck a guitar string.

Anything that vibrates makes the air around it vibrate. When the air vibrates, it creates sound waves in the air. Usually you can't see any vibrations when you hear a sound, but the vibrations are still there. Sound vibrations travel through most other materials, as well as through air.

60

How do we hear sound?

When sound waves enter your ears, they make the insides of your ears vibrate. Inside each ear is a sheet of cells called the eardrum. The sheet is stretched tight, like the skin across the top of a drum. When the sound waves hit the ear-

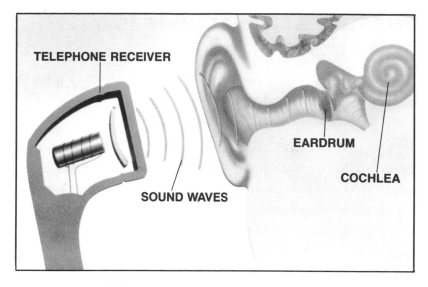

drum, the eardrum begins to move quickly, or vibrate, the way a drum does when it is hit. These vibrations cause three tiny bones in the ear to vibrate, too. The bones' vibrations, in turn, cause vibrations in a liquid that fills the deepest part of the ear. The moving liquid presses on your hearing nerve cells, which pass the message on to your brain, and the sound is heard!

Why are some sounds low and others high?

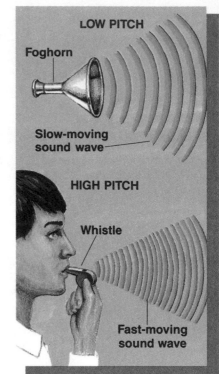

LOW PITCH

Foghorn

Slow-moving sound wave

HIGH PITCH

Whistle

Fast-moving sound wave

The sound coming from a vibrating object will be high or low depending on how many sound waves it makes each second. The highness or lowness of sound is called pitch. A low sound, like that made by a foghorn, has slow-moving waves. A high sound, like that made by a whistle, has fast-moving waves. The lowest sounds that most people can hear have about 20 vibrations each second. The highest sounds people can hear have about 20,000 vibrations per second. Some animals, such as bats and dolphins, can hear very high sounds—those with more than 100,000 vibrations per second. The scientific word for the number of vibrations per second is *hertz*. It is abbreviated hz. People can hear sounds between 20 and 20,000 hertz.

"SOUND TRAVELS FASTER IN WATER THAN IN AIR"

© 1987 United Feature Syndicate, Inc.

"IN AIR, SOUND TRAVELS ONE MILE IN FIVE SECONDS"

ALL RIGHT, WHO LEFT THE LID OFF THE GRAPE JELLY?!

SLIGHTLY SLOWER THROUGH FLANNEL.

2-23

Do sound waves behave differently if it is cold or wet outside?

Yes. Temperature and water affect how fast sound waves can travel. The speed of sound is slower in cold air and faster in warm air. Sound waves that travel in water may move four times faster than they would in air. Think of that! Although water would slow you down if you were trying to run in a pool, sound waves move faster in a pool. Sound waves that travel through solids move about 15 times faster than they would through air!

What are echoes?

Echoes are sounds made by reflected sound waves. If you stand near the wall of your school gym and clap your hands, you hear the sound of the clap. In a moment, you may hear the sound again. That's the echo.

You hear the first sound instantly, as sound waves travel from your hands to your ears, but sound waves travel in many directions at the same time. Some reach the gym wall, bounce off it, and return to your ear as reflected sound—the echo.

Can echoes be bad?

Echoes can be annoying in auditoriums or concert halls. Sometimes when an orchestra or band is playing, many echoes travel in all directions. The reflected sound that mixes with the original sound can form one continuous sound. If this happens, the music will sound muffled or unclear, as if you were wearing a hat pulled over your ears. Some concert halls pad the seats, walls, and floors to absorb, or take in, some of this reflected sound. Then, the audience hears only the original sound made by the orchestra.

How does a band shell use reflected sound?

Some outdoor theaters have been built so that they make use of reflected sound with band shells. They are designed in such a way that the reflected sound is sent directly back to the audience. This way the sound is not lost. Instead, the sound is amplified (AM-pluh-fied), or made louder.

A symphony orchestra performs in the band shell at the Hollywood Bowl in California.

63

Sound Waves at Work

How does a stethoscope help a doctor listen to your heart?

A stethoscope lets the doctor listen with both ears. Before stethoscopes were invented, a doctor had to listen to a heart by pressing one ear against the patient's chest. Now doctors hear heartbeats better by using both ears.

A stethoscope has two listening pieces to help the doctor hear different kinds of sounds. The small disk piece is good for listening to very low-pitched sounds. The large disk piece is good for listening to higher sounds. The sounds travel from the listening pieces through rubber tubes to the doctor's ears. The next time you go for a checkup, ask the doctor to let you listen to your heart with the stethoscope.

CAN I LISTEN, TOO?

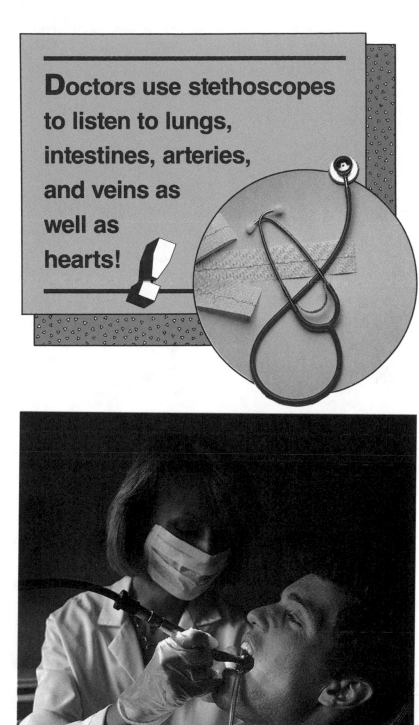

Doctors use stethoscopes to listen to lungs, intestines, arteries, and veins as well as hearts!

Can doctors use sound to see inside your body?

Yes. Doctors use sound called ultrasound. Ultrasound vibrates above the 20,000 hertz region, where we can't hear. These sound waves can be sent into the human body. The sound waves travel through liquids such as blood and water differently than through solids such as bone and muscle. Doctors can look at the different organs inside the body when the waves form an image, or picture, on a special screen. Doctors use ultrasound to make sure an unborn baby is growing in a healthy way inside its mother.

How do dentists use ultrasound?

Dentists can use ultrasound to clean teeth. An ultrasonic scaler vibrates to remove hard deposits, called tartar, on the teeth. Who ever thought that teeth could be cleaned using sound?

CHAPTER 9

Strike up the band. We're ready to hear the blare of the trumpets, the call of the bugle, and the rat-tat-tat of the drum! Join the *Peanuts* marching band and orchestra for a music lesson that can't be beat! There will be lots of instruments to read about along the way.

MUSIC TO YOUR EARS

THE SOUND OF MUSIC

How do musical instruments make sounds?

All musical instruments make air vibrate, but they don't all do it in the same way. Some have strings that vibrate. Others have small pieces of wood, called reeds, that vibrate. With some instruments, the vibrations come from the player's lips. Drums, cymbals, and xylophones (ZIGH-luh-fones) vibrate when somebody strikes them.

Most musical instruments are made so that the player can control how high or low the sound will be.

PIANO

How does a piano make sounds?

Most pianos have 88 keys. There are 52 white keys and 36 black keys. Attached to every piano key is a hammer. This is a piece of wood covered with a felt pad. When you press a key, the hammer hits a small group of metal strings. Most pianos have 230 strings.

The pitch of each string depends on how long and thick the string is and how tightly it is stretched. Short, thin strings have a higher pitch than long, thick strings. The tighter you stretch a string, the higher its pitch will be. Some of the strings are wrapped with wire to make them vibrate more slowly, which creates lower sounds.

PLAY IT AGAIN, SCHROEDER.

In 1935, a giant-sized piano was built in London. Its longest string was 9 feet long. That's probably more than twice your height!

GUITAR

How does a guitar make music?

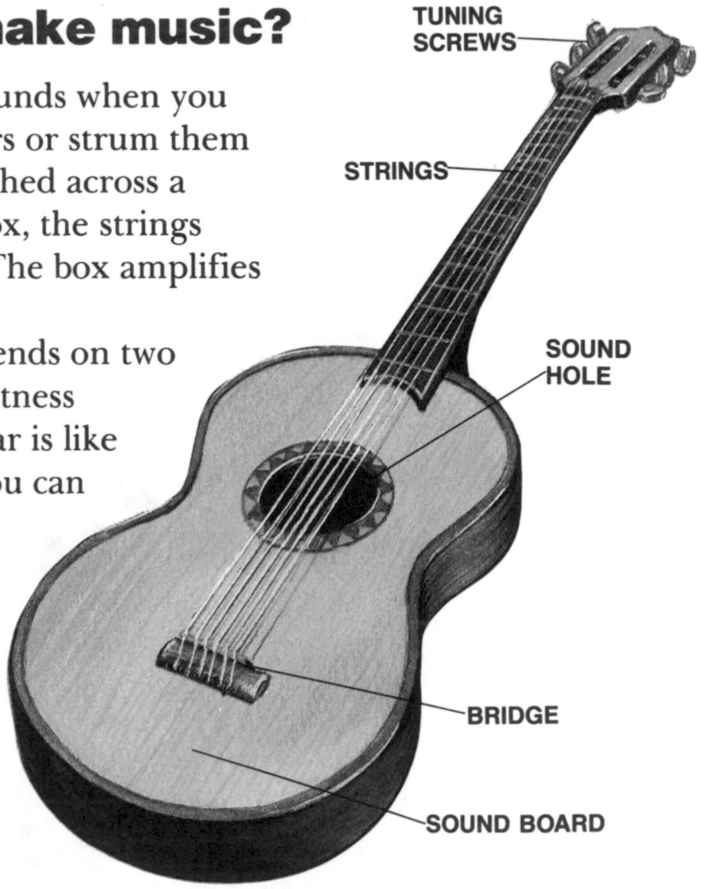

TUNING SCREWS

A guitar has strings that make sounds when you pluck the strings with your fingers or strum them with a pick. The strings are stretched across a pear-shaped box. Without this box, the strings would make a very faint sound. The box amplifies the sound, makes it louder.

STRINGS

The pitch of a guitar note depends on two things: the thickness and the tightness of the strings. In that way, a guitar is like a piano. On a guitar, however, you can change the pitch by pressing a string with your finger. When you do this, you are cutting short the part of the string that vibrates. In a way, you are making the string shorter. Banjoes and ukuleles (you-kuh-LAY-leez) work in much the same way.

SOUND HOLE

BRIDGE

SOUND BOARD

VIOLIN

Does a violin work the same way as a guitar?

Not quite. A violin has strings like a guitar. When you play a violin, you control the pitch by pressing on the strings—as you do with a guitar. Instead of plucking the strings to make them vibrate, however, you rub a bow across the strings. The bow is a wooden stick with horsehairs stretched between the ends. Sound vibrations are made when the hairs rub on the violin strings. Some violinists may occasionally pluck the violin strings like those of a guitar to get interesting sounds.

Imagine playing a violin under water! Mark Gottlieb did it as a stunt in 1975 in Olympia, Washington. He played Handel's *Water Music!*

WIND INSTRUMENTS

What is a wind instrument?

A wind instrument is any instrument that makes a sound when someone blows into it. A horn, a kazoo, and a saxophone are all wind instruments.

A wind instrument has a body made of a long or short tube. When you blow into the instrument, air vibrates inside the tube. The longer the tube, the lower the pitch. Most wind instruments have push buttons on, or holes in, the tube. That's where you put your fingers when you play the instrument. When you press a button or uncover a hole, the pitch changes because the space left for the air to vibrate in changes.

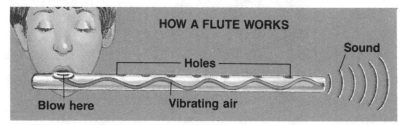

HOW A FLUTE WORKS

Holes

Sound

Blow here   Vibrating air

There are two main kinds of wind instruments. They are called brass and woodwind.

PEANUTS MARCHING BAND

70

What are brass instruments like?

Bugles, trumpets, cornets, trombones, tubas, French horns, and sousaphones are brass instruments. They all have long tubes that are folded or curled around to make the instrument easier to carry. Brass instruments are made of brass.

When you play a brass instrument, you press your lips together and make a buzzing sound like "p-f-f-f-t" as you blow into the tube. When you go "p-f-f-f-t," your lips vibrate. This makes the air in the instrument vibrate. The pitch of the sound depends on how quickly or slowly you vibrate your lips.

How are woodwind instruments played?

Woodwind players blow air across one or two thin pieces of wood called reeds. Clarinets, oboes, bassoons, and saxophones are played this way. Blowing makes the reeds, and then the air, vibrate. Woodwind instruments without reeds—flutes and piccolos—have a hole in the mouthpiece that the player blows air across. Blowing across the hole makes the air inside the instrument vibrate. Once, all woodwinds were made of wood. Today, some are made of plastic or metal.

PERCUSSION INSTRUMENTS

What is a percussion instrument?

Percussion instruments are usually struck with sticks, the hand, or mallets to make music. The entire instrument may vibrate, as do cymbals, or part of it may vibrate, as does the skin on the top of a drum.

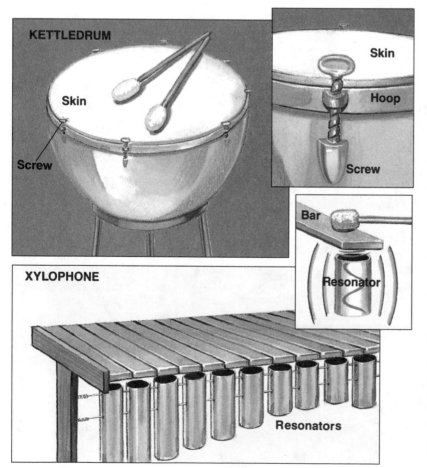

KETTLEDRUM

Skin

Screw

Skin

Hoop

Screw

Bar

Resonator

XYLOPHONE

Resonators

How do they make sound?

When a cymbal is hit, the sound can only be made louder or softer; the pitch cannot be changed. The pitch is changed on a drum by tightening or loosening the skin. Xylophones are instruments with lots of bars. When the bars are struck, a sound is made. The longer the bar, the deeper the sound.

CHAPTER 10

Your eyes need it to see. A camera needs it to take photographs. Movies need it to move. Doctors need it to see inside your body. What is *it*? It's wonderful light!

LIGHTS, CAMERA, ACTION!

DIRECTOR

LIFE OF
LUCY
TAKE 27

LIGHT AND HOW WE SEE IT

What is light?

Light is a form of energy. Like sound, light travels in waves. Light waves vibrate like sound waves, and can have different speeds of vibration. Instead of letting us hear different pitches, however, light waves allow us to see a whole world of different colors.

Each color of light has its own length of wave. Red light waves are long, violet ones are short. The light waves for other colors are in between those two.

Is it true that your eye is like a camera?

Yes, it's true. A camera has a diaphragm (DIE-uh-fram), a ring or plate that gets bigger or smaller to let in the right amount of light. Your eye has an iris that does the same thing. A camera has a lens that focuses the light into a clear picture. Your eye also has a lens to focus the light. In a camera, the light helps to form a picture on film. In your eye, the picture is formed on the retina (RET-ih-nuh), at the back of the eye. The picture is upside down on both the film and on your retina.

How do you see?

You see with your eyes, and also with your brain. First, waves of light pass into your eye and form an upside-down picture on your retina. The retina has special nerve cells on it. When the light hits these cells, they send a "picture message" to your brain. Your brain interprets the message into a right-side-up picture—and you see.

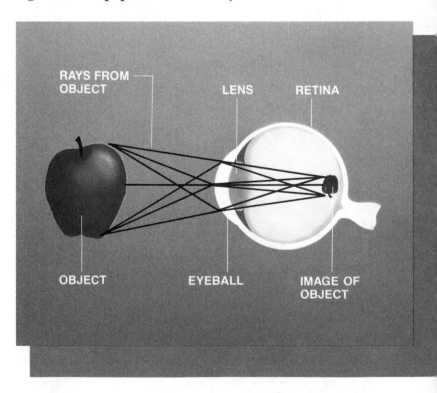

RAYS FROM OBJECT   LENS   RETINA

OBJECT   EYEBALL   IMAGE OF OBJECT

74

How do eye-glasses and contact lenses help people see better?

When light waves enter the eye, they pass through the curved front end called the cornea. Then they pass through the lens. The cornea and the lens of the eye focus, or aim, the light waves so that the picture on the retina will be clear. Some people's eyes cannot do this very well. If an eyeball is too long or too short from front to back, the image will be blurry.

Eyeglasses and contact lenses are extra lenses put in front of the eyes' own lenses. They focus or bend the light waves. Then the waves come together correctly in the eye and form a clear picture.

This painting shows Benjamin Franklin and his invention, bifocals.

How are bifocals different from other eyeglasses?

Regular eyeglasses have one simple lens for each eye. The lens helps a person see either nearby things better or faraway things better. Bifocals have one lens with two parts for each eye. One part helps a person see nearby things better. The other helps a person see faraway things better.

Benjamin Franklin invented bifocals in 1785. Before that time, people who needed glasses to see both faraway and nearby things clearly had to carry around two pairs. With bifocals, however, such people need only one pair of glasses.

75

LIGHT AT WORK

How does a camera make photographs?

A camera works very much like an eye. Light waves enter the front of a camera through a set of lenses. The lenses focus the light to form a picture on the inside back wall of the camera. To make photographs, you need a roll of film. Photographic film is a strip of plastic coated with special chemicals that change when light hits them. The camera is made to hold part of the roll of film against the back wall of the camera. When you press the shutter release, light comes into the camera. The light waves shine on the film. They change the chemicals so that a picture will appear when the film is developed.

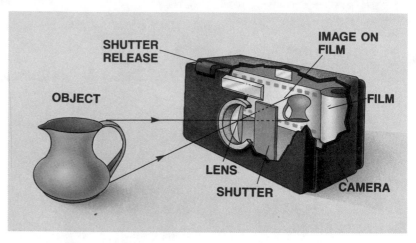

How is film developed?

When you take your film to be developed, the person you give it to sends it to a laboratory. There, the film is taken into a darkroom and unrolled. The developing has to be done in the dark because light would ruin your pictures. The film is dipped into a tank of liquid chemicals. These chemicals change the colors of the chemicals on your film in such a way that pictures are formed. These pictures are called negatives. A negative shows the objects in the picture with the right shapes but the wrong colors. If black-and-white film is used, the blacks will appear white, and the whites will appear black. If color film is

COLOR NEGATIVE

used, the colors will be very different from those in the finished photograph.

Next, each negative is placed in a machine called an enlarger. The enlarger holds the negative and shines light through it for a few seconds, projecting the picture onto a piece of photographic paper. Photographic paper is coated with chemicals on one side. The paper remains blank, but the light causes invisible changes in the chemicals.

Next, the paper is placed in a pan of liquid chemicals. These liquids change the chemicals on the paper. Slowly, as the chemicals change, the picture appears, and your photograph is finished.

BLACK AND WHITE
NEGATIVE

How can X rays take a picture of a person's insides?

X rays are like light waves, but they are much shorter and have greater energy. Scientists have built machines, called X-ray machines, that shoot beams of X rays, just as flashlights shoot beams of visible light. When light waves hit a person, they bounce off. When X rays hit a person, however, they go right through—just as light goes through a piece of glass. Light waves and X rays behave differently when they hit a person, but when either light waves or X rays hit a piece of photographic film, they behave the same. Both kinds of waves change the chemicals on the film. To make an X-ray picture of a person's insides, an X-ray machine shoots rays through the person onto a piece of photographic film. Like the sound waves used in ultrasound pictures, X rays travel differently through the liquid and solid parts of the body. When the film is developed, it shows a shadowy picture of the bones and other organs inside the body.

SOME PEOPLE ARE BEAUTIFUL INSIDE AND OUT.

The man who discovered X rays, Wilhelm Roentgen (RENT-gun), didn't understand what they were. That's why he called the rays *X!* X is a common mathematical symbol for an unknown!

78

What is a CAT scanner?

A CAT scanner is a special kind of X-ray machine. CAT is a word made from the initials of the words Computer Assisted Tomography. A person who is going to have a CAT scan is placed into the machine, which looks like a giant tube. The X-rays from the CAT scan shoot through the person onto a screen, and then the tube is turned a little. More X-rays are sent through the body. Then the machine turns again. The machine continues to scan until it finally gets back to its starting place. Regular X-rays just shine waves through one side of a person. The CAT scan shines rays through a person in a complete circle. Because so much information is gathered by a CAT scan, a computer must be used to help make sense out of the hundreds of pictures it takes. These CAT scan pictures are much clearer than those produced by regular X-ray machines.

Today, machines like the MRI (Magnetic Resonance Imagery) and PET (Positron Emission Tomography) scans are even more sophisticated. They can actually watch the way the brain works—and they can pinpoint exactly where a problem lies.

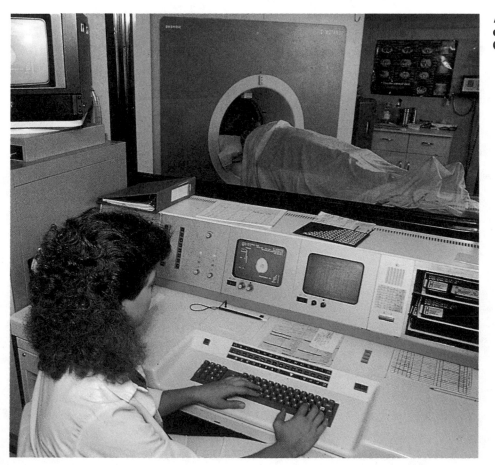

A technician operates a CAT scanner.

79

MOVIES AND CARTOONS

What makes movies move?

If you look at a piece of movie film, you can see that it is just a long series of photographs on a plastic strip. Each photograph is a tiny bit different from the one just ahead of it and the one behind it. If the film is of someone running, jumping, or diving, you can see that the arms and legs are in different positions in different pictures. When you show the film in a projector, the projector flashes the pictures on a screen one at a time, but they flash on very fast—usually 24 pictures per second. When the pictures flash by that fast, your brain can't tell that your eyes are looking at many separate photos. You think you are looking at only one picture—a picture that moves.

A-choo! Here's a strip of film showing a sneeze.

Who invented movies?

No one knows for sure. In the 1880s and 1890s, many people were working on ways to make moving pictures. In 1891, Thomas Edison, the inventor of the light bulb, built the first kinetoscope (kin-ET-uh-scope). This was a cabinet with a peephole. Inside were reels of film that turned. A person looked into the peephole to see the movie. Some people believe that Edison's helper, Thomas Dickson—not Edison— invented the kinetoscope.

THOMAS EDISON AND HIS KINETOSCOPE

How are cartoon movies made?

Cartoon characters are just drawings, and they can't move. It is possible, however, to play a trick on people's eyes so that it looks as if they are moving. This is called animation. To create animation, artists draw thousands of pictures on a computer or by hand on separate clear plastic sheets called cels. Each picture shows a character in a slightly different position.

For each scene, the artists paint a background. One or more cels are put on top of the background. The combination is photographed by a special movie camera, which takes only one picture each time a button is pressed. (A regular movie camera keeps taking one picture after another.) Then the cels just photographed are taken off the background. The next picture is placed on the background. It is only slightly different from the first picture. The second picture is then photographed. In fact, one picture is taken for each tiny bit of movement a character makes. When the film is shown through a movie projector, the characters appear to move.

Cartoon movies can also be made with puppets. They can be animated by moving their bodies in a slightly different position for each picture.

CHAPTER 11

What travels faster than sound and comes in all the colors of the rainbow? The answer is right before your eyes—light! With the help of prisms, mirrors, and magnifying glasses, light can do some incredible things. Just watch!

A CHANGE OF DIRECTION

PRISMS

Sunlight creates a wide range of colors when it passes through a prism.

What is a prism?

A prism is a bar of glass with flat sides. A good prism has no bubbles or ripples in it. When a beam of sunlight passes through a prism, the light spreads out into separate beams of color. The colors are the same as those you would see in a rainbow—red, orange, yellow, green, blue, indigo, and violet. A rainbow in the sky is created when light passes through drops of water in the air that act as prisms. Like a prism, a drop of water can change sunlight into separate colored beams of light.

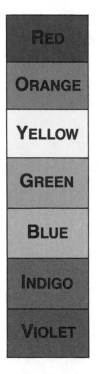

RED

ORANGE

YELLOW

GREEN

BLUE

INDIGO

VIOLET

How does a prism cause a rainbow?

A beam of sunlight is really a mixture of light waves of many colors. As we've already learned, each color of light has its own kind of wave. Red light waves are long, violet light waves are short, and the other colors are in between.

When light waves enter a prism, they bend, and they bend again when they come out of the other side of the prism. The various colors bend by different amounts. Because of this, the colors spread out as they pass through the prism. The colors line up side by side in the order shown here.

THIS IS A REPORT ABOUT A BUNCH OF BAD LIGHT WAVES WHO WERE SENT TO PRISM...

MIRRORS AND MAGNIFYING GLASSES

Why does a mirror show a picture of what's in front of it?

A mirror shows a picture, called a reflected image, because the mirror has a shiny, silver-colored coating behind the glass. The coating does two things:

1. It keeps the light waves from passing through the mirror. Since they can't go through, they bounce back toward your eyes.

2. It makes the mirror *very* shiny. When light waves bounce off a dull surface, they scatter. When the light waves bounce off something shiny, however, they don't scatter at all.

When you stand in front of a mirror, light waves move from you to the shiny mirror. The light waves then bounce right back off the mirror in exactly the same way they hit the mirror. And you see yourself!

How does a magnifying glass make things look big?

A magnifying glass plays a trick on your eyes. It does this by changing the direction of light waves coming from the object you are looking at. The curved surfaces of the magnifying glass bend the waves, and it appears to your eyes that the waves are coming from a big object.

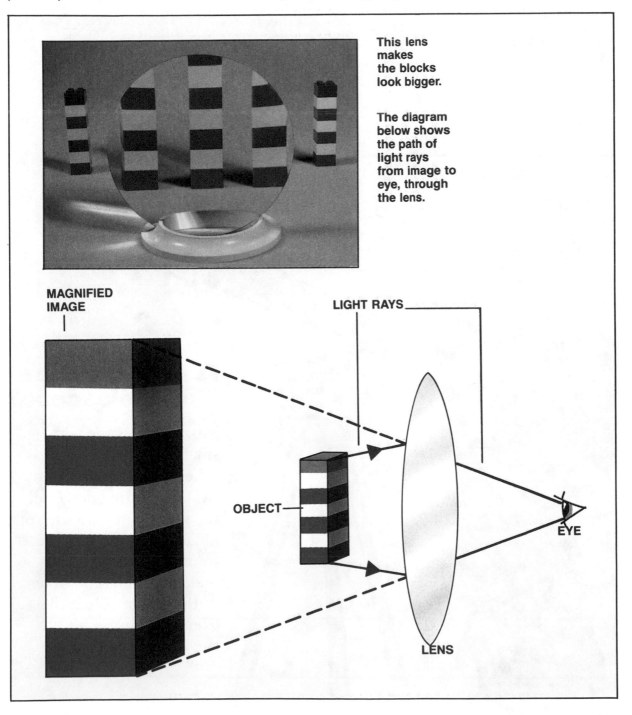

This lens makes the blocks look bigger.

The diagram below shows the path of light rays from image to eye, through the lens.

MAGNIFIED IMAGE

LIGHT RAYS

OBJECT

LENS

EYE

TELESCOPES AND MICROSCOPES

How does a telescope work?

By using a series of lenses, the eyepiece of the telescope makes distant objects look closer. The lenses in the telescope let us see faraway objects that are normally invisible. In fact, the telescope can make these objects appear as if they were right next to us. We can even see planets that are two billion miles away!

GEE, I THOUGHT THE BIG DIPPER WAS A LARGE ICE CREAM SCOOP.

Is a microscope like a telescope?

Yes. It lets us see very small objects that would otherwise be invisible to us. Unlike the telescope, the microscope focuses on objects that are very close to us. One set of lenses makes an enlarged image of the object. Then the eyepiece lenses enlarge the image further.

LASERS AND HOLOGRAMS

What is a laser?

A laser is a machine that shoots a thin, very high-powered beam of light. This beam is called a laser beam. Some laser beams are so powerful that they can burn holes in metal.

Here's a colorful laser light show.

How does a laser work?

A laser beam comes from a laser tube. Light is a form of energy, and, as we know, it travels in waves or ripples. Ordinary light waves spread out in all directions because the ripples are all jumbled. A laser unjumbles the waves and packs them side by side so that they all travel together. When light waves are packed together, they travel in a straight line instead of spreading out. These light waves make up a laser beam.

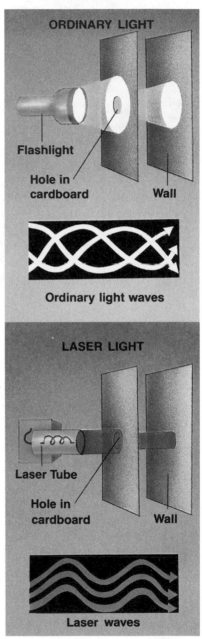

ORDINARY LIGHT vs. LASER LIGHT

ORDINARY LIGHT

Flashlight

Hole in cardboard

Wall

Ordinary light waves

LASER LIGHT

Laser Tube

Hole in cardboard

Wall

Laser waves

The flashlight beam and laser beam *both* go through the hole in a piece of cardboard, but the laser beam does not spread out.

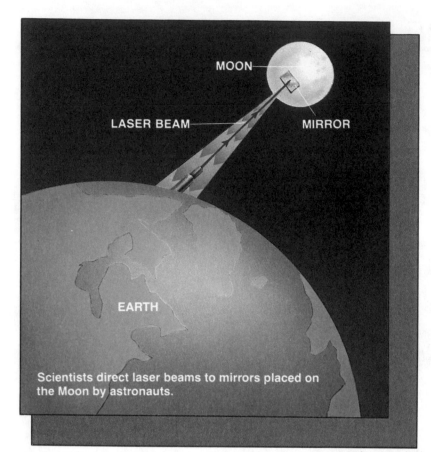
Scientists direct laser beams to mirrors placed on the Moon by astronauts.

How do people use lasers?

Many uses have been found for lasers. Laser beams are much hotter than other light beams. Their heat can be used to weld or cut tiny things. Sometimes surgeons use a laser to perform delicate operations.

Laser beams can travel farther than other light beams. Scientists can measure how far it is from Earth to the moon by bouncing a laser beam off the moon.

What is a hologram?

A hologram is a picture that appears to have depth—just like the real object. When you see a normal picture, it looks flat. When you look at a hologram, the object looks so real you want to reach out and touch it! Holograms are made with lasers and photographic plates or film. You might find a hologram on a decal, in a magazine, or on one of your parents' credit cards.

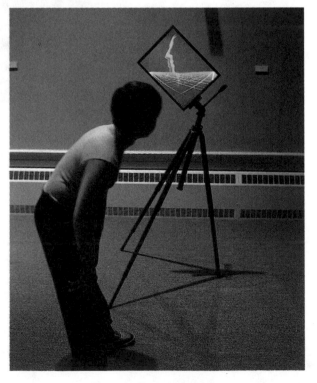
This boy is looking at holographic art created with lasers.

CHAPTER 12

You can't see it, and you can't touch it, but you can move through it. Sound and light waves travel through it, too. It's all around us, and it's called air. What is air? Charlie Brown and the *Peanuts* gang are here to reveal the mystery and magic of marvelous air.

THE AIR AROUND US

THE NATURE OF AIR

What is air?

Air is made up of gases. Gases are made up of very small particles called molecules. Molecules are always moving in different directions, bumping into things, but they are invisible to us. The two gases that make up most of the air are nitrogen and oxygen. Without the right amount of both gases, it would be difficult to breathe.

What happens when air molecules bump into each other, or collide?

When air molecules collide with walls or with each other, they create a force, or pressure. Air in a sealed box creates pressure against the walls of the box. If we make the box smaller, there are more collisions of air molecules, and the pressure increases.

CHANGING THE AIR'S TEMPERATURE

What is heat?

Heat is a form of energy. When we heat up air, we speed up the movement of the gas molecules. When we cool down air, we slow down the molecules.

How does a furnace make a whole house warm?

When coal, gas, or oil is burned inside a furnace, heat is produced. The heat can be moved from the furnace to other places in a house in at least three different ways:

1. The furnace can heat the air. A blower pushes the warm air from the furnace through tunnels called ducts. The ducts lead to openings in all parts of the house.

2. The furnace can heat water in a boiler. When the water boils, it turns to steam. The pressure of the steam makes it go through pipes to radiators in each room.

3. The furnace heats water in a boiler. A pump then sends the hot water through pipes to radiators. When the radiators become hot, they warm the air in the rooms.

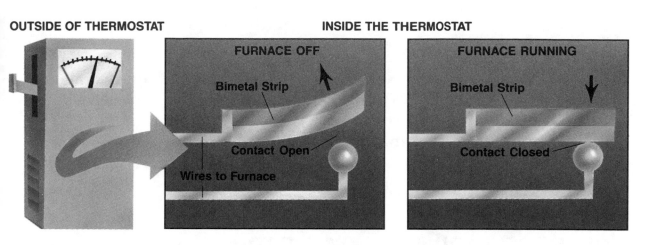

OUTSIDE OF THERMOSTAT

INSIDE THE THERMOSTAT

FURNACE OFF

Bimetal Strip

Contact Open

Wires to Furnace

FURNACE RUNNING

Bimetal Strip

Contact Closed

What makes a furnace turn on and off by itself?

Furnaces in houses and other buildings are controlled by thermostats (THUR-muh-stats). A thermostat turns the furnace on when the building is cool, and off when the building is warm. A thermostat has a bimetallic (by-muh-TAL-ick) spring made of two metal strips. *Bimetallic* means made from two metals.

When the room temperature rises, one of the metal strips winds up tighter than the other, and the spring stretches in one direction, turning off an electric switch. When the temperature falls, the spring stretches in the other direction, turning the switch back on.

HEY, WHO TURNED OFF THE HEAT?

What other things use thermostats?

Many things that work by heating or cooling use thermostats. Refrigerators, air conditioners, ovens, electric frying pans, and electric blankets all have thermostats. If you set an air conditioner's thermostat at 75 degrees Fahrenheit, it will keep the temperature of the room fairly steady. As soon as the air gets cooler than 75 degrees, the air conditioner shuts off. As soon as the air gets warmer than 75 degrees, the air conditioner turns on again.

How does a radiator warm a room?

A hot radiator warms the air next to it. The warmer the air gets, the lighter it becomes. Light air rises, so the warm, light air rises toward the ceiling. However, that does not leave airless space near the floor by the radiator because the gap is instantly filled by cool air that moves in from other parts of the room. This cool air becomes warm next to the radiator, and then *it* rises. The rising of the warm air and the movement of cool air toward the radiator is called convection (kun-VECK-shun). Convection is like a tiny wind that spreads the heat of the radiator all through the room.

What is solar heating?

Solar heating uses energy that comes from the sun. In recent years, oil and gas have become expensive. People have also realized that the burning of coal and oil pollutes the air and uses up natural resources that can never be replaced. So scientists and inventors have been searching for new ways to heat houses. One way is to capture heat from sunshine. Even in winter, a lot of heat comes to us in the form of waves from the sun. The problem is how to catch this heat energy and bring it indoors before it gets away.

How can people catch the sun's heat?

The most common solar heat collector is a low, flat box with a glass or plastic window on top. Most of the sun's light waves can pass easily through the glass or plastic. The inside of the box is painted black, because dark colors absorb, or soak up, the incoming light waves. Light colors reflect the waves.

The collector box is placed outdoors, usually on a roof facing the sun. The box is sealed tightly so that none of the heat that enters can get away. When the sun is shining, the box becomes hot inside, even in winter.

The next step is to bring the heat from the box into the house, using water pipes and a pump. Cool water is pumped from the house to pipes inside the collector box. The heat in the collector warms the water in the pipes. A pipe takes the hot water back into the house, where it is used. Sometimes the water goes into a storage tank, but if it stays there too long, it gets cold. Then it is pumped back up to the box to be reheated.

How does a dryer take the water out of wet laundry?

Wet clothes become dry because the water that is in them evaporates (ih-VAP-uh-rates). When water evaporates, it changes to water vapor, a kind of gas, and goes off into the air. A clothes dryer is a machine that makes evaporation take place quickly. It does this by blowing air on the clothes while they are tumbling around. Usually the air is warmed by a gas flame or an electric heater. This makes the water in the clothes evaporate quickly. Heat makes the tiny particles of water jump into the air. The moist air is then blown out of the dryer.

THERE'S NOTHING QUITE LIKE A WARM BLANKET, FRESH FROM THE DRYER.

Labels in diagram:
COOLING COILS • INSULATION LAYERS • HEAT ESCAPES • COLD AIR • THERMOSTAT • DOOR GASKET • PLUG • COMPRESSOR

STAY COOL!

JOE COOL

What makes a refrigerator cold inside?

A refrigerator is a machine for taking heat out of a closed box. The working of a refrigerator is based on one special fact: a liquid absorbs, or soaks up, heat when it evaporates. When a liquid evaporates, it changes into a gas.

A refrigerator has a metal tube filled with a liquid called a refrigerant that evaporates fast. Part of the tube is inside the food box, and part of the tube is outside—underneath the refrigerator or on the back. If the inside of the food box gets warm, a thermostat turns on the refrigerator's motor. This makes the liquid flow through the tube. When the liquid enters the part of the tube that is *in* the food box, the liquid evaporates. It soaks up heat. Because the liquid has evaporated, the tube leading out of the food box is filled with gas. The tube leads to a compressor (come-PRESS-ur). A compressor pumps the gas into a condenser (cun-DEN-sir). As the gas flows through the condenser, it is changed into a liquid, and it gives off heat, so the condenser becomes hot. The heat goes into the air of the kitchen as the liquid moves through the part of the tube outside the refrigerator. The liquid again enters the food box. There, it evaporates and soaks up more heat.

How does an air conditioner make a room cool?

An air conditioner works exactly the same way as a refrigerator, but instead of taking heat out of a food box and putting it into the kitchen, an air conditioner takes heat out of a room and puts it outdoors.

Part of a room-sized air conditioner is inside a window. This part has a cold tube filled with a cooling liquid refrigerant. Part of the air conditioner is outside the window. This part has a compressor and a condenser tube that gives off heat. An air conditioner also has a fan that blows air past the cold tube and out into the room. In this way, an air conditioner takes the hot, humid air out of the room and returns cool, dry air to the room.

CHAPTER 13

W hat keeps the milk in your thermos cold and the hot chocolate warm? And what keeps your bicycle tires just right? The answer to the first question is: no air. The answer to the second question is: lots of air. Let's see why!

NO AIR AND LOTS OF AIR

Vacuums

What is a vacuum?

When air is pulled out of a space so that no air is left, the empty space is called a vacuum (VACK-yoom).

How does a thermos bottle keep milk cold?

Thermos is a brand name for a vacuum bottle. A vacuum bottle works by insulating (IN-suh-late-ing) whatever you store in it. This means that when you store something cold, like milk, the bottle lets in very little heat. When you store something hot, like cocoa, the bottle lets very little heat get out.

A vacuum bottle is built like a bottle inside of another bottle. There is a narrow space between the two bottles where the air has been pumped out to form a vacuum. The vacuum keeps air from touching the inside bottle. It is important to have no air between the two bottles. Air can carry heat to cold things and take heat away from hot things.

Some heat can get through a vacuum, but much of this heat is blocked by the bottle's shiny, silvery coating. Heat, which travels in waves, bounces off shiny, silvery things.

CLOSE-FITTING STOPPER

SILVERED WALLS

VACUUM

COLD OR HOT DRINK

SUPPORT

How did the vacuum cleaner get its name?

When a vacuum cleaner is turned on, a fan keeps blowing out most of the air from its tank. A space with only a little bit of air inside it is called a partial (PAR-shul) vacuum. As the air goes out of a vacuum cleaner's tank, a partial vacuum is left. That is why we call it a "vacuum" cleaner.

How does a vacuum cleaner pick up dirt?

It uses suction. The vacuum cleaner's fan blows air out of its tank or bag, leaving a partial vacuum inside. If you make an opening in the side of the container of a vacuum or partial vacuum, air will rush in to fill the empty space. This is called suction.

Along with the air that rushes into a vacuum cleaner come dust and dirt. The air is blown out again, but the dust and dirt are caught in the dust bag, which is made of paper or cloth. When the bag is full, you can throw it away or empty it and reuse it.

SORRY, PIGPEN. WE CAN'T PLAY INSIDE TODAY. MY MOTHER JUST VACUUMED.

COMPRESSED AIR AT WORK

How does a scuba-diving tank work?

The scuba tank holds compressed air. *Compressed* means that a lot is squeezed into a small space. If you let all the air out of a scuba tank, it could fill a whole room. On the tank, a special knob, called a valve, lets a little bit of air at a time go from the scuba tank through a hose to the diver's mouth.

The most important parts of a scuba outfit are the valves. They control the amount of gas or liquid that goes through a pipe or hose. Some valves are like faucets. They start or stop the flow of liquid or gas when you turn them with your hand. A special kind of valve in a scuba outfit automatically lets the diver get more air when he goes down deep. Another special valve lets the diver breathe used up air out into the water. It also doesn't let any water come in when the diver breathes in.

Who invented modern scuba equipment?

Ocean scientist Jacques Cousteau invented scuba gear.

It was invented in 1943 by Jacques Cousteau (ZHOCK koo-STOE), the famous French ocean scientist who has made many nature films for television. He didn't invent it all by himself, however. He had a partner named Emile Gagnan (ay-MEAL gah-NYAH). The two men made a perfect team. Cousteau was an ocean diver in the French navy. Gagnan was an engineer who knew a lot about valves.

Cousteau knew that old-fashioned diving equipment was unsafe. Often divers couldn't get enough air when they went down very deep. He saw that a new kind of valve was needed to control the amount of air coming from the scuba tank. Gagnan made the kind of valve Cousteau wanted.

What does scuba mean?

Scuba is an acronym made from the initials of the words *self-contained underwater breathing apparatus.*

What makes a fire extinguisher squirt?

Some fire extinguishers use compressed air to squirt out the water inside. As soon as the compressed air is given room, it will spread out. When a fire extinguisher is turned on, the compressed air pushes the water out the opening, which leads to a hose. The air goes out through the hose and pushes the water out.

Other fire extinguishers use compressed gas to make them squirt. The gas for most extinguishers, carbon dioxide, is pumped in at the factory. One type of extinguisher, however, makes compressed gas when you turn it upside down. This type is called a soda-acid extinguisher. The soda in soda-acid is not the kind you drink. It is a chemical called baking soda. The acid is a chemical called sulfuric (sull-FYOOR-ick) acid. The extinguisher is filled with water. Soda is dissolved in the water. In the top of the extinguisher is a small bottle of sulfuric acid. When you turn the extinguisher upside down, the acid mixes with water and baking soda. As a result, a lot of carbon dioxide gas is formed. It is under pressure inside the extinguisher until you let it out.

SO WHERE'S THE FIRE?

How does a fire extinguisher put out fires?

Fires need two things to keep going: a gas called oxygen, and fuel. Fuel is anything that can get hot enough to burn. Some extinguishers cool the fuel. Others keep oxygen in the air away from the fuel.

Extinguishers that squirt water work mostly by cooling the fuel until it is too cool to burn. Extinguishers that squirt carbon dioxide make the fuel very cold—colder than ice. They also drive oxygen away from the fire. Some extinguishers squirt a dry chemical powder. It forms a crust on the fuel. The crust keeps oxygen away from the fuel. Another type of extinguisher coats the fuel with foam. The foam keeps oxygen away from the fuel.

Rock can be broken with the help of a jackhammer.

What machine is used to chop holes in the pavement?

Jackhammer, air hammer, and pneumatic (new-MAT-ick) drill are all names for the machine used to chop holes in sidewalks.

A jackhammer runs on compressed air. The air is pumped into the jackhammer through a hose. A trigger in the handle controls the flow of air.

Inside the jackhammer is a hollow tube called a cylinder (SILL-in-dur). Inside the cylinder is a piece of metal called a piston. The piston can slide up and down inside the cylinder.

When the jackhammer is turned on, air comes into the top of the cylinder. It pushes the piston down very hard. The piston then slams into a chisel that sticks out of the bottom of the jackhammer. The chisel is a pointed, metal bar. The hard blow of the piston drives the chisel into the pavement.

Next, the air comes into the *bottom* of the cylinder and pushes the piston back up. When the piston reaches the top of the cylinder, the air changes direction again. The piston goes down and slams into the chisel again. The piston goes up and down more than 1,000 times a minute! Each time the chisel chops away a piece of pavement.

How does a bicycle pump work?

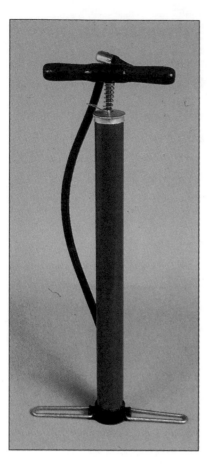

A bicycle pump compresses air. One common kind is made up of a handle, a cylinder, a valve, a hose, and a metal disk with a gasket around it. A gasket is a ring that fills an open space to make a pump or pipe leakproof. A gasket is sometimes made of rubber and sometimes of metal.

When you pull up on the handle of a bicycle pump, two things happen. First, the gasket hangs down loose and limp. This lets air go past it into the lower part of the cylinder. Second, the valve closes, so the air stays squeezed inside the bottom of the cylinder.

When you push down on the handle, the gasket presses tightly against the cylinder, making a tight seal. The air cannot get back up past the disk, but compressed air wants to spread out. Where can it go? When you push down on the handle, the valve opens. The air rushes out through the valve into the hose and then into your bicycle tire.

How does a car's brake pedal stop the car?

When a driver steps on a brake pedal, a chain of events begins. The pedal pushes a lever. The lever pushes a piston in a cylinder full of liquid. The piston pushes the liquid into four hoses. Each hose leads to one of the four wheels of the car. The liquid flows into a cylinder next to each wheel. There, the liquid pushes more pistons. These pistons push flat plates of metal against discs of metal called brake rotors. The rotors are attached to the wheels of the car. The plates of metal have layers of friction material called brake pads. The friction, or rubbing, of the pads slows down the turning of the wheels so that the car slows down and stops. When the brake pedal is released, the pads stop rubbing against the brake rotors.

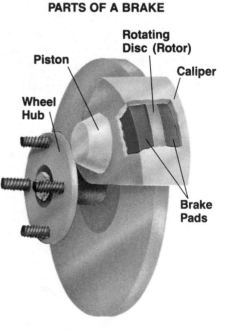

PARTS OF A BRAKE

Rotating Disc (Rotor)

Piston

Caliper

Wheel Hub

Brake Pads

Do trains have the same kind of brakes as cars?

Not exactly. Trains need very powerful brakes—much more powerful than brakes controlled by the pressure of one person pushing on one pedal with one foot. Train brakes use compressed air. The compressor is in the front of the train's locomotive. Hoses take the air to all the wheels. When the driver puts on the brakes, compressed air rushes into the hoses. The air pushes against some pistons. These pistons push curved pieces of metal against the wheels to slow down or stop their turning.

Big trucks use the same kind of brakes as trains.

What makes a car-lifting machine go up and down?

You have probably seen the machine used in service stations to lift a car into the air. It has a big, shiny metal tube that comes up out of the floor. That metal tube is really a giant piston. The piston fits into a pipe or cylinder buried in the floor. When the mechanic wants to lift the car, he turns on a pump. This pump uses compressed air to force liquid into the cylinder. The rising liquid pushes the piston up. When the car is raised high enough, the mechanic closes a valve. This keeps the liquid in the cylinder. The liquid keeps the piston from sliding back down into the floor. Then the mechanic turns off the pump. Now it is safe for him to go under the car and fix it. The car can't fall as long as liquid stays in the cylinder. When the mechanic wants to let the car down, he opens the valve. The liquid slowly leaves the cylinder and goes into a storage tank. As the liquid leaves the cylinder, the piston slowly sinks to the floor.

WHY WOULD ANYONE WANT TO WHISPER?

• Imagine a room shaped like an egg! People have built elliptical, or egg-shaped, rooms because of what such rooms do to sound. In these rooms, a person can whisper at one end, and someone standing in a special spot across the room can hear very clearly what is being said. People standing anywhere else in the room cannot hear the whisper at all! The Statuary Hall of the U.S. Capitol was built like this and is called the "whispering gallery."

• The average light bulb lasts for 750 to 1,000 hours. A light bulb made by the Shelby Electric Company in 1901 still burns when switched on, almost 90 years after first being turned on.

...AND NOW, MY IMPRESSION OF A BEAGLE.

• Have you ever put your hands in front of the light of a movie projector and made funny rabbit and alligator shadow figures? Those shadows show us that light travels in straight lines. When your hand blocks the light, it creates a shadow. If light traveled in curves, it would curve around your hand, and you would see no shadow at all.

WHO'S THE STUPID KID WHO KEEPS LOOKING AT US THROUGH THE WINDOW?

IF HE HAS A ROUND HEAD, I MAY KNOW HIM..

• There's a world of light and color inside a kaleidoscope (kall-EYE-duh-skope). This long tube is filled with loose scraps of colored glass, plastic, or paper. What makes a kaleidoscope magical, however, are the angled mirrors inside. When light shines on them, the mirrors reflect a pattern of color that changes every time the colored pieces move. If you want to see a new pattern, all you need to do is turn the kaleidoscope!

• The Pontiac Silverdome is a Michigan sports stadium with an amazing roof. It's held up by air pressure! Five pounds per square inch support the Fiberglas™ roof.

• Did you ever wonder how whipped cream comes out of the can? Inside a spray can is compressed gas. The compressed gas is always pushing at the cream, but it can't rush out until you push the button on top of the can. Pressing the button is like opening a faucet. You give the compressed gas a place to go. As the gas rushes out, it pushes out the whipped cream. The fancy ridges come from the can's star-shaped nozzle.

• People who visited the Washington Monument on July 17 and 18 in 1987 were treated to a super sound event. David Frank of Toronto, Canada, whistled there for 35 hours—nonstop!

THAT'S MUSIC TO MY EARS!

Can you imagine a world without television and cassette players? Or what would everyday life be like without light bulbs and refrigerators? Or can you picture life without the telephone? A wonderful form of energy makes all these things work. It's the power of electricity and magnetism.

INVISIBLE ENERGY

CHAPTER 14

THE NATURE OF ELECTRICITY

What is electricity?

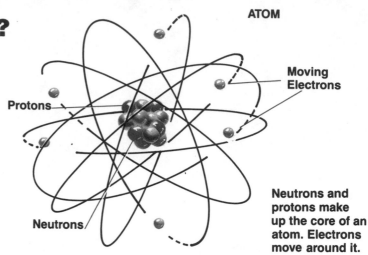

ATOM

Protons →

Moving Electrons

Neutrons

Neutrons and protons make up the core of an atom. Electrons move around it.

Electricity is a form of energy. In order to understand electricity, you have to know something about atoms. Atoms are the tiny, tiny bits of matter that all things are made of. Atoms are so small that you can't see them even with the most powerful microscope. Though atoms are so small, they are made of even smaller parts. Some of these parts are called electrons (eh-LECK-tronz). When electrons move around among the atoms, a current of electricity is produced. In some materials, the electrons are loosely attached to the atoms. This makes it easy to break the electrons loose so they can move to other atoms. Electrons are loosely attached in all metals. That is why people use metal wires to carry electricity from one place to another. We say that these wires are good conductors, or carriers, of electricity.

What is static electricity?

When electrons do not move in a current, or flow, but get stored up, that's static electricity.

Sometimes when you walk across a rug, then touch a doorknob, you feel a small shock. Electrons move from the rug to your body and escape when you touch the doorknob. Then you feel the shock.

I'VE GOT IT FIGURED OUT, SIR.. WINTERGREEN CANDY MAKES SPARKS BECAUSE OF ELECTRICAL CHARGES..

WELL, CHEW HARDER.. I'M TRYING TO READ THIS MAP..

I DON'T THINK I HAVE ANY TEETH LEFT..

SCHULZ

What is an electric shock?

An electric shock is what you feel when a current of electricity passes through your body. A strong shock, as from a light socket, can cause burns or even kill a person. A weak shock can sting your skin and make your muscles jerk.

Shocks are no fun, so here are some "nevers" to remember. Never touch electric things when they are wet, or if your hands are wet, and don't touch them if you are standing in water. Water is a good conductor, so wetness increases your chances of getting a bad—even a fatal—shock. *Fatal* means "causing death." Never climb telephone poles, and keep away from signs saying "Danger High Voltage." Stay away from electric wires lying on the ground. You don't have to be afraid of electricity. Just be careful with it.

Why are electric wires covered with plastic or rubber?

The plastic or rubber insulates (IN-suh-lates) the wire. This means it keeps the electricity from leaking out through the sides of the wire. An insulated wire is safe to touch. A bare wire can shock or even kill a person who touches it. Sometimes when a wire is old, the insulation cracks and starts to peel or break off. Spotting this is not always easy, but when it happens, someone might easily get a shock, or a fire might start. If you see a wire with cracked insulation, tell a grown-up so that the wire can be replaced.

What is a watt?

A watt is the unit used to measure electric power. A 100-watt light bulb uses 100 units of electric energy every second. A 60-watt light bulb uses 60 units of electric energy every second. In either case, electric energy is changed into heat and light energy. The watt is named after James Watt, the man who invented the steam engine.

What is an electric motor?

An electric motor is a kind of machine that is powered by electricity. The motor changes electric energy into movement that can do work. For example, an electric mixer has a small motor inside it. When the mixer is plugged in and the motor switch is turned on, the motor starts to spin. It causes the beaters to spin, too. The beaters then can mix up batter for a yummy cake.

How does electricity make toasters and electric irons get hot?

When a toaster or electric iron is turned on, an electric current flows through a coil of wire. This means that electrons are moving along among the atoms that make up the coil of the toaster or iron. As the electrons make their way, they bump into atoms. This bumping changes the energy of the current into heat energy. The coil becomes hot. Other appliances that use electricity to heat are electric coffeepots and hair dryers.

MAGNETISM AND ELECTROMAGNETS

What is a magnet?

A magnet is something that can attract iron. It can make a nail or a paper clip move toward it and then stick to it. A bar of iron or steel is an example of a simple magnet. Sometimes the bar is bent into the form of a horseshoe.

A magnet's attraction is strongest at its ends, or poles. Every magnet has a north pole and a south pole. If you hold two magnets near each other, the north pole of one will be attracted to the south pole of the other. If you try to bring the north pole of one magnet together with the north pole of another, they will repel, or push against, each other. This also happens with two south poles. Opposite poles attract each other. Poles of the same kind repel.

What do magnets have to do with electricity?

A lot. Magnetism and electricity are close relatives. In fact, electricity can produce magnetism, and magnetism can produce electricity.

A magnet has an invisible field, or area, of magnetic force around it. This is the area where the magnet's "pulling power" works. A wire with electricity running through it has the same kind of invisible magnetic field around it and the same kind of pulling power.

You can show the shape of a magnet's invisible field. Put a magnet under a piece of paper. Then sprinkle powdered iron on top of the paper. (You can probably get powdered iron at a hobby shop.) Now tap the paper gently. The iron will move into a pattern around the magnet. This pattern gives you a clear picture of a part of the magnet's invisible force field.

THIS WILL SHOW YOU THE MAGNET'S INVISIBLE FORCE FIELD, SIR.

Do some magnets run on electricity?

Yes. They are called electromagnets. You can make a small electromagnet by winding lots of thin copper wire around an iron nail. Use wire that has a protective covering. Scrape off about an inch of the covering at each end of the wire. Attach the ends to a battery. You will have to have a friend hold the ends of the wire against the ends of the battery. It would be best to use the kind of battery called a lantern battery. You can get this kind of battery in a hardware store.

An electric current flows from the battery through the wire to the nail. The nail becomes magnetic. Now that it is magnetized, the nail can pick up other things made of iron.

If you disconnect the wire from the battery, the nail loses almost all of its magnetism.

The world's biggest magnet is 196 feet wide and weighs 40,000 tons!

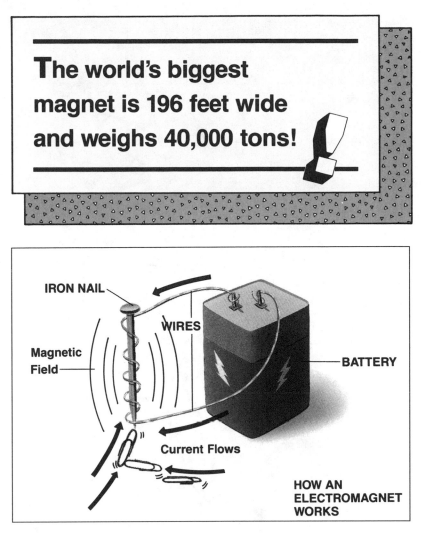

IRON NAIL
WIRES
Magnetic Field
BATTERY
Current Flows

HOW AN ELECTROMAGNET WORKS

Are electromagnets better than ordinary magnets?

In at least one way, yes. When an electromagnet is turned on, you can lift a heavy iron object and move it to any place you want. As soon as you shut off the electricity, the electromagnet will stop working. Then it will drop the iron.

You could not do this with an ordinary magnet. An ordinary magnet keeps holding on to iron things. That's why it is sometimes called a permanent magnet. *Permanent* means lasting forever. If you want to separate a piece of iron from a permanent magnet, you must pull it off.

This crane uses an electromagnet to lift junked metal.

How are electromagnets used?

Big electromagnets are often used in junkyards to load scrap iron into railroad cars. They are also used to separate iron from other kinds of scrap, such as aluminum, copper, or glass. Small electromagnets are used to make some machines work. For example, a doorbell uses an electromagnet.

CHAPTER 15

They can be lighter than a dime or too heavy to lift. They can be round, square, or shaped like a tube—and you can find them just about everywhere you look. They're in watches, the family car, flashlights, calculators, and many of your toys! What are they? Batteries!

CHARGE UP YOUR BATTERIES

BATT

ROBO-MAN

BATTERIES

I THINK IT NEEDS A NEW BATTERY.

What is a battery?

A battery is something that produces an electric current with the help of different types of chemicals.

You've probably seen the type of battery that goes inside a portable radio or a flashlight. It looks something like a small can. This can and everything inside it is called a dry cell. Some batteries are made up of one dry cell. Others use two or more. Inside the cells are all the chemicals and other things needed to produce electric current.

The chemicals in dry cells are in the form of jellies or pastes. They can't be spilled. That's why these cells are called dry cells. There are also cells called wet cells. The chemicals inside these are liquids. Some batteries, called storage batteries, can be recharged and used over and over again. One kind of wet cell, a storage battery, is used to start a car. It is made of three or six cells in a heavy rubber or plastic box.

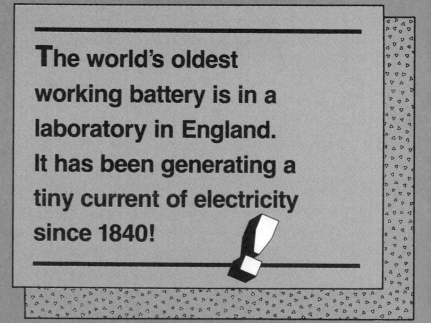

The world's oldest working battery is in a laboratory in England. It has been generating a tiny current of electricity since 1840!

How does a battery produce an electric current?

Batteries produce currents by a chemical reaction. Usually, a cell of a battery has three chemicals. One, called the electrolyte (eh-LECK-troe-lite), causes the other two to react. When the two chemicals react, the electrons in their atoms do a lot of moving around. One chemical ends up with a load of extra electrons. Another chemical ends up with a shortage of electrons. In this way, these two chemicals become what is called electrically charged. The chemical with extra electrons gets a negative, or minus, charge. The chemical with a shortage of electrons gets a positive, or plus, charge. When the chemicals are electrically charged, the electricity is ready to flow out of the battery.

In order for the flow to begin, there must be a complete path for the current to follow. Such a path is called an electric circuit (SIR-kit). A circuit is like a closed loop. When electrons travel along a circuit, they eventually go back to the place where they started. The electrons move around the circuit by using energy given to them by the battery. As you see in picture 1, the light bulb goes on when the circuit is complete. In picture 2, the light bulb does not go on because the circuit is broken.

What makes batteries go dead?

When a battery can no longer produce current, we say it is dead. A battery stops producing all current when its chemical reaction stops. The reaction stops when some of the chemicals have been used up.

Can a dead or weak battery be made to work like new again?

Ordinary flashlight batteries can't be renewed, but certain other batteries can. These are called storage batteries. Renewing a battery is called recharging it. Cars have rechargeable batteries. Some small vacuum cleaners, calculators, tape recorders, portable phones, and toys run on rechargeable batteries.

How are car batteries recharged?

Car batteries recharge automatically when the car's engine is running. The engine is connected to a type of generator, called an alternator. (We'll see how generators work in the next chapter.) The generator forces a current to run backward through the battery. This means the new chemicals change back into the old chemicals. The chemicals can react again to generate more electricity. Recharging is what allows the battery to keep starting the car every day for years.

CHAPTER 16

The flow of billions and billions of tiny electrons helps light our cities, heat our homes, cook our food, and clean our clothes Where does the flow of these electrons begin? Let's go with Charlie Brown and the *Peanuts* gang to find out.

GOING WITH THE FLOW

ELECTRIC CURRENTS

Huge plants like this hydroelectric plant generate enough power to light up whole cities.

Where do electric currents come from?

Most of the electric currents that people use come from batteries or from machines called generators. The current that runs the lights, the TV, the refrigerator, and other things in your house probably comes from a very large generator in a place called a power plant.

What is a generator?

A generator is a machine that makes electric current flow. A generator can be smaller than your big toe or bigger than your living room. A small generator can power a bicycle's headlight. A large one can give power to a whole city.

How does a generator produce an electric current?

A generator changes one form of energy into another. Every generator is run by something that turns or spins. The turning wheel of a bicycle runs the generator that powers its headlight. The spinning wheel or blades of a large engine run the generator. In the generator, the spinning energy is turned into electric energy. Here's how.

The people who make generators keep certain scientific facts in mind.

1. Around every magnet is an invisible force field.
2. If you move a coil of copper wire past a magnet, the wire cuts across the force field.
3. When the force field is cut by the wire, electricity flows through the wire.

Inside a generator are magnets (often electromagnets) and a coil of wire. The wire is usually wrapped around a rod called an armature (ARM-uh-choor). The engine that runs the generator moves the armature. As long as the armature keeps moving, the magnet's force field is cut. As long as the magnet's force field is cut, a current of electricity is produced, or generated.

POWER PLANTS

What is a power plant?

A power plant is a place where large amounts of electric energy are generated. There are at least seven different kinds of power plants. All of them have generators. The energy to run the generators, however, comes from different sources—oil, coal, atoms, water, gas, or wind.

The three most common kinds of plants are steam-electric plants, hydroelectric (hy-droe-ih-LECK-tric) plants, and atomic or nuclear (NOO-klee-ur) plants.

The Hoover Dam uses water to make electrical energy.

How does a steam-turbine plant work?

A steam-turbine plant uses steam to spin a turbine. The spinning motion of the turbine runs the generator that produces the electric current.

Steam is made by burning fuel to boil water. A huge amount of water is boiled to make steam. A steam-run plant is like a giant teakettle with steam blowing out the spout. The steam goes through a tunnel. Inside the tunnel are wheels with blades. This tunnel of blades is the turbine.

When steam blows through the tunnel, it makes the blades spin. The rod they are mounted on spins also. The rod is connected to the electric generators. When it spins, the generators run.

124

How does a hydroelectric power plant generate electricity?

A hydroelectric power plant uses a water-powered turbine to run a generator. The water comes from a reservoir (REZ-ur-vwar) or a lake. Most of it is held back by a large wall called a dam. Gravity, the force that pulls everything downward, makes some water flow through tunnels from the top of the dam to the bottom. Just before the water is let out at the bottom of the dam, it runs through the turbines and makes them turn. Flowing water can turn turbines just as wind can turn windmills or pinwheels. When turbines spin, they make the generators spin, and electric currents are produced.

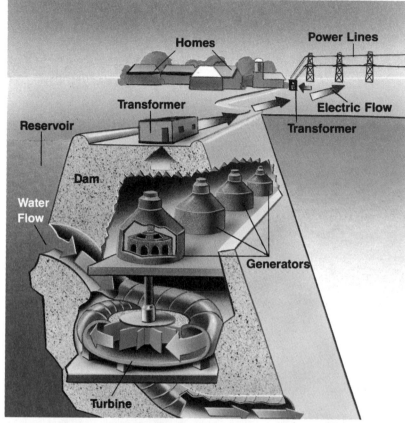

The world's largest hydroelectric power plant can make enough electric energy to turn on 64 million 100-watt light bulbs!

How does an atomic power plant generate electricity?

An atomic power plant works almost the same as a steam-turbine power plant does—it heats water. An atomic plant, however, doesn't burn coal, oil, or gas. Instead, it uses the metal uranium (you-RAY-nee-um) to make heat for boiling water. Instead of burning the uranium in a furnace, the uranium is put into a nuclear reactor. There, the atoms that make up the uranium split and produce huge amounts of nuclear energy. In doing this, a great amount of heat is given off. The heat turns the water to steam. The steam blows through tur- bines, and the turbines turn the generators.

Huge cooling towers are needed at this nuclear power plant in France.

BRINGING ELECTRICITY INTO HOMES

How does an electric current go from a power plant to people's houses?

It leaves the power plant through thick, heavy wires called transmission (tranz-MISH-un) lines. The current is sent out under high electrical pressure, or at high voltage. The lines are held up by tall metal towers.

Transmission lines stretch for miles. When they come to a town where people need electricity, some of the lines go into a place called a substation. The substation changes the high-voltage electricity into low-voltage electricity, which is safer. The low-voltage electricity then goes through wires from the substation to a transformer. This makes the voltage even lower. From there, it travels to houses, factories, and offices.

The same person, Michael Faraday, invented the electric motor, the generator, and the transformer!

PSYCHIATRIC HELP FEATURING LUCY

THE PSYCHIATRIST IS [IN]

I LOVE SEEING MY NAME UP IN LIGHTS!

What is a brownout?

Sometimes the area around a power plant needs more power than usual. This often happens in the summer, when people are using air conditioners. Sometimes one power district can buy power from a neighboring power district. Special cables are set up to make this possible.

If your power district cannot buy enough power from a neighbor, it may send out power to your home at a lower voltage. This is called a brownout.

If the voltage is reduced just a little, you won't notice it. If it is reduced 5 percent or more, your lights will be dimmer. Some appliances, such as your toaster and your iron, might not work as well as usual.

What is a blackout?

When the power plant stops sending electricity to your neighborhood, you have a blackout. During storms, if power lines are knocked down, you may have a blackout. Or, the power company may stop sending electricity to your area in order to send power to other places during a shortage. If something goes wrong at the power plant, there may be a blackout until the problem is fixed.

During a blackout, you can't watch TV or listen to the radio or stereo (unless yours run on batteries). Your refrigerator stops working, and if you have an electric stove, your parents aren't able to cook.

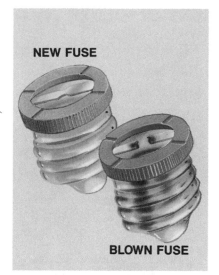

NEW FUSE

BLOWN FUSE

When a fuse filament melts, it breaks the connection and cuts off the flow of electricity.

A BLACKOUT! DOES THAT MEAN SUPPER IS OFF?

What does a fuse do?

It protects your house from fires caused by electric currents that are too large. All electric current that comes into your house must pass through the fuse. If you take the fuse out, the circuit is broken. No electricity comes in. If you put the fuse back, your house has current again.

Inside the fuse is a piece of metal. If this piece of metal gets too hot, it melts very quickly. Melting is the way it protects your house.

For example, suppose you are using an air conditioner, a TV, a toaster, and all the lights in your house. Then you turn on the microwave oven. You are now causing too much current to go through the circuit in your house. The wires become very hot, and they could start a fire. However, before this can happen, the metal piece in the fuse melts from the heat. We say that the fuse blew. Electrons can no longer flow through the wires of your house, so an electrical fire cannot start. In order to get electric current flowing into your house again, you must put in a new fuse.

Do circuits in all buildings have fuses?

No. Fuses are becoming old-fashioned. Newer buildings have circuit breakers instead. On the outside, circuit breakers look like ordinary light switches, but on the inside, a circuit breaker has a spring that bends when it gets hot. The spring will get hot if too much current is going through the circuit. If the spring gets hot and bends, the circuit breaker will flip to the off position. The current shuts off. After you wait a few minutes for the spring to cool, you can flip the circuit breaker back on. First, though, you should turn off some of your appliances. Then the circuit breaker probably won't switch off again.

How does the electric company know how much to charge each customer?

Each customer's house or apartment has a meter that measures how much electric energy the customer uses. The numbers on the dial tell the company's meter reader how many kilowatt-hours of electric energy the customer has used. A kilowatt is a unit of electric power. One kilowatt is equal to 1,000 watts. If you use a 1,000-watt iron for an hour, then you have used one kilowatt-hour of electricity. If you keep a 100-watt bulb burning for ten hours, that also adds up to one kilowatt-hour. The meter keeps track of every little bit of electric energy that is used, and it all adds up to a certain number of kilowatt-hours. Each month, a person from the electric power company comes to your house to read the numbers on your electric meter. This is how the company finds out how much power you have used. If you want to save money and energy, be sure to turn off lights, TVs, and other appliances when you're not using them.

CHAPTER 17

A BRIGHT IDEA

Flashlights, headlights, night-lights, traffic lights. Lights in your house, in your school, on streets, and on highways. Without a doubt, lights make our world a brighter, safer—and more enjoyable—place to live!

LEMONADE
5¢ A GLASS

LIGHT BULBS

What makes the light go on when you flip a switch?

When you flip a switch, you complete an electric circuit. As long as the electrons keep flowing, the bulb stays lit. If you break the circuit by turning off the switch, the flow of electrons stops. Then the light goes out.

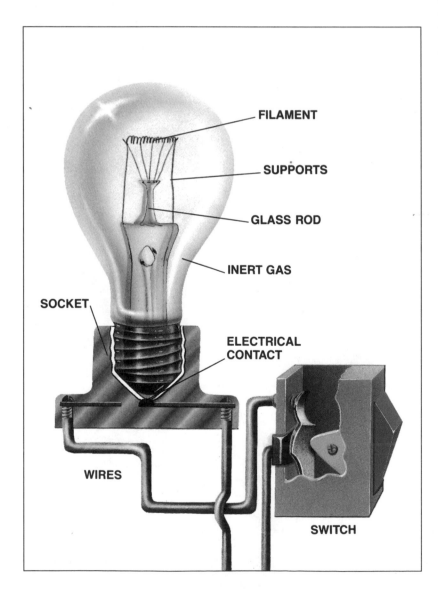

FILAMENT

SUPPORTS

GLASS ROD

INERT GAS

SOCKET

ELECTRICAL CONTACT

WIRES

SWITCH

What makes a light bulb light up?

Inside a light bulb is a thin wire called a filament (FILL-uh-munt). When electricity passes through the filament, the filament becomes very hot. It becomes so hot that it glows and gives off a bright white light. The filament reaches a temperature of about 4,500 degrees Fahrenheit. The glass part of a light bulb keeps air from reaching the filament. It is important to keep air away from the filament because air has oxygen (OCK-suh-jin) in it. Oxygen is one of the three things needed to start a fire. The other two are heat and fuel, or something that can burn. A white-hot filament has the heat and is burnable. If any oxygen happened to reach a hot filament, it would burn up in an instant.

It takes a switch, a socket, and wires to light a bulb.

132

What makes light bulbs burn out?

When a light bulb stops working, we say that it has "burned out," but it really hasn't burned. What really happened was that the bulb's filament broke. When the filament breaks inside a light bulb, electrons can't pass through it. When electrons can't pass through the filament, then the filament can't get white-hot and glow.

The oldest working light bulb has been burning in a firehouse in California since 1901!

Heat can make the filament break. Heat causes tiny cracks to form in the filament. The more you use the bulb, the bigger the cracks become. Finally, one of the cracks will stretch all the way through the filament, and the filament will break apart.

Who invented the electric light bulb?

Thomas Edison, in 1879. He was one of the greatest inventors who ever lived. If you ask people to name some important inventors, usually the first one they will think of is Edison. His most famous inventions were the electric light bulb, the phonograph, and a motion picture machine called a kinetoscope (kih-NET-uh-scope). Altogether, he and his helpers invented more than 1,000 things.

Thomas Edison pictured in his laboratory

Thomas Edison's first electric light bulb glowed for 40 hours before it burned out!

MA'AM? THOMAS EDISON, HE WAS A MAN WITH A BRIGHT IDEA.

What is the difference between a light bulb and a fluorescent lamp?

The most obvious difference is their shape. A light bulb usually has a round or pear shape. A fluorescent (flow-RESS-unt) lamp usually has a tube shape. However, that is not the only difference.

In a light bulb, light is made with a glowing hot filament. In a fluorescent lamp, the glow comes from a special white coating (phosphor) on the inside of the glass tube. The coating glows whenever certain invisible rays, called ultraviolet (UL-truh-VYE-uh-lit) rays, hit it. These ultraviolet rays are made when you turn on the electricity. When the lamp is on, electrons shoot from one end of the tube to the other. The tube is filled with a special gas that gives off ultraviolet rays whenever electrons shoot through it. Fluorescent lamps save money because they use less electric power than light bulbs do.

What makes flash bulbs flash?

Oxygen. Flash bulbs have oxygen sealed inside. When you press the button on your camera, electric current flows through the bulb's filament. The filament glows. However, the glow doesn't last the way it does in an ordinary light bulb. This is because the oxygen makes the filament burn up in a flash of bright light. This flash gives you a lot of light in enough time to snap a picture.

Many modern cameras use a sealed glass tube that can flash over and over again and never wears out or burns out. This tube is called a strobe.

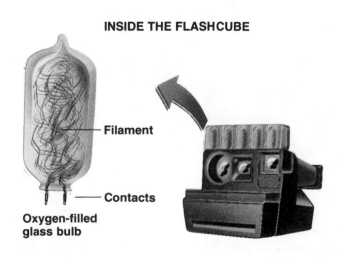

INSIDE THE FLASHCUBE

— Filament

— Contacts

Oxygen-filled glass bulb

CHAPTER 18

SAY HELLO WITH ELECTRICITY

Hundreds of years ago, people who lived far away from each other could not talk to one another. Letters had to travel by horse-back or boat, which could take days or even weeks. For shorter distances and faster delivery, they sent coded messages using flashing mirrors or smoke signals. Now, because of electricity, spreading important news is as easy as dialing a telephone.

THE TELEGRAPH

Does electricity help people send messages?

Yes. If you want to contact someone far away, and you want to do it quickly, you can use a telegraph, a telephone, a cellular car phone, a CB radio, or even a fax machine. All these methods use electric energy.

What is a telegraph?

A telegraph is the oldest method of using electricity to send and receive messages. Samuel F. B. Morse invented the telegraph in 1837. For the first time, people could contact each other instantly between any two places that could be connected by wires. Before the telegraph, messages had to be sent by mail or by private messenger. The telegraph is no longer used much. It has been replaced by telephones and radios.

Samuel Morse demonstrates his invention, the electric telegraph.

How does a telegraph work?

Besides wires and batteries, a telegraph system has a sender, called a key, and a receiver, called a sounder. An operator works the telegraph.

The key is really just a switch the operator presses to make a current from a battery flow through the wires. When the operator stops pressing, the current stops. The sounder has an electromagnet that moves an iron lever when the current is on. When the lever moves, it taps or clicks against another piece of iron. The clicks are either long or short. Different patterns of clicks stand for different letters. The receiving operator listens to the clicks and can understand the message being sent. This system using clicks to stand for letters is called Morse code.

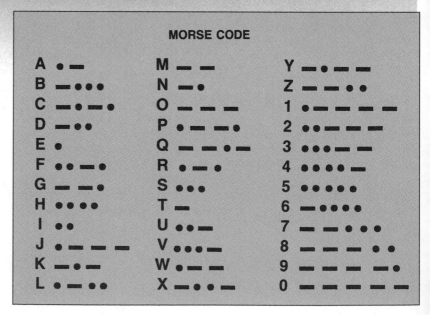

Do people still use Morse code?

Not usually. But a code much like Morse's is still used by radio operators. Instead of clicks, the radio code uses short and long beeps, called dots and dashes. If you know someone who operates a radio as a hobby, maybe you can listen to people sending messages in code. If you learn the code, you will understand what they are saying.

MORSE CODE		
A ● ▬	M ▬ ▬	Y ▬ ● ▬ ▬
B ▬ ● ● ●	N ▬ ●	Z ▬ ▬ ● ●
C ▬ ● ▬ ●	O ▬ ▬ ▬	1 ● ▬ ▬ ▬ ▬
D ▬ ● ●	P ● ▬ ▬ ●	2 ● ● ▬ ▬ ▬
E ●	Q ▬ ▬ ● ▬	3 ● ● ● ▬ ▬
F ● ● ▬ ●	R ● ▬ ●	4 ● ● ● ● ▬
G ▬ ▬ ●	S ● ● ●	5 ● ● ● ● ●
H ● ● ● ●	T ▬	6 ▬ ● ● ● ●
I ● ●	U ● ● ▬	7 ▬ ▬ ● ● ●
J ● ▬ ▬ ▬	V ● ● ● ▬	8 ▬ ▬ ▬ ● ●
K ▬ ● ▬	W ● ▬ ▬	9 ▬ ▬ ▬ ▬ ●
L ● ▬ ● ●	X ▬ ● ● ▬	0 ▬ ▬ ▬ ▬ ▬

Can you read this?

•••• • •—•• •—•• ———
_H_ _e_ _l_ _l_ _o_

••—• •—• ——— ——
_F_ _r_ _o_ _m_

—•—• •••• •—• •—•• •• •
_c_ _h_ _a_ _r_ _l_ _ie_

—••• •—• ——— •—— —•
_B_ _r_ _o_ _w_ _n_

Write your name here, using Morse code.

Was there any fast way to send messages between America and Europe before telephones were invented?

Yes. In 1866, a heavy wire called a cable was laid across the bottom of the Atlantic Ocean. This cable made it possible for people to send telegraph messages between America and Europe. Before the cable was laid, messages had to go by ship. This meant that people didn't know what was happening on the other side of the ocean until days or sometimes even weeks later.

Now there are cables under all the world's oceans. They carry telephone messages and other electronic signals.

The longest undersea cable runs more than 9,000 miles from Australia to Canada!

139

THE TELEPHONE

How does a telephone work?

Every time you talk, you start sound waves moving through the air. When you talk on the telephone to a friend, the sound waves from your voice enter the part of the phone called the mouthpiece. The sound waves flow against a paper-thin piece of metal called a diaphragm (DYE-uh-fram). They make it vibrate, or move back and forth very quickly.

As the diaphragm vibrates, it jiggles tiny bits of carbon in a small box attached to it. The carbon bits move in time with the vibrations of your voice.

An electric current flows over the telephone wires between your house and your friend's house. The action of the carbon bits changes the strength of the electric current that goes over the wires. The current is strong when the carbon bits bunch together. It is weak when they spread apart. As a result, the spurts of current follow the same pattern as the sound waves from your voice.

When the spurts of current reach your friend's house, they must be changed back into the sound of your voice. In your friend's phone (and in yours, too) is a small electromagnet. When the spurts of current reach the electromagnet, another thin, metal diaphragm begins to vibrate. This diaphragm is in the part of the phone called the earpiece. The vibrations set sound waves in motion. The sound waves reach your friend's ear, and your friend hears you say "Hello!"

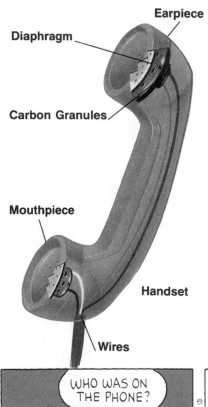

Earpiece

Diaphragm

Carbon Granules

Mouthpiece

Handset

Wires

WHO WAS ON THE PHONE?

A GIRL WHO SAID SHE WAS AN OLD FRIEND OF YOURS CALLING FROM OUT OF THE BLUE...

I DIDN'T KNOW WHERE THAT WAS SO I HUNG UP..

© 1989 United Feature Syndicate, Inc.

7-20

There are about 400 million telephones in the world! More than a third of them are in the United States!

SAY, DID YOU HEAR THAT CLICKING NOISE?

YEAH, CHUCK. WHAT DO YOU THINK IT IS?

The average American makes about 1,800 telephone calls each year!

Alexander Graham Bell invented the telephone in 1876 while trying (without success) to invent a hearing aid for deaf people!

HEE, HEE, HEE! I LOVE LISTENING ON THE EXTENSION!

THE RADIO

How does a radio work?

Radio is a way of sending voices and music through the air instead of along electric wires. It's like a wireless telephone. In fact, when radio was first invented, people called it the wireless. Instead of wires, radio uses electromagnetic waves. These waves can travel through air—and even through great distances in space.

Who invented the radio?

Guglielmo (goo-lee-YELL-moh) Marconi (mar-KOE-nee) invented the radio in 1895, when he was 21 years old. Marconi became very interested in science when he was a boy. He began experimenting when he was 16. For a long time, scientists had said it should be possible to make a radio—or wireless telegraph, as it was called—but nobody could figure out how to do it. Marconi studied other scientists' ideas and experiments. Then, when he was 20, he tried to invent a radio on his own. He built a transmitter that could send telegraph messages to a receiver across his attic—all without wires!

Then Marconi successfully sent signals across his father's vegetable patch at home. Later he was able to send messages across England and the English Channel. In 1901, Marconi achieved an even greater goal: he sent the letter *S* in Morse code across the Atlantic, all the way from England to Newfoundland! Marconi's invention ushered in the amazing age of radio.

Guglielmo Marconi

142

Early radio makers broadcast their own programs. If they hadn't, no one would have had a reason to buy a radio. There were no other programs to listen to!

RADIO WAVES

How are radio waves made?

Radio waves are made by a transmitter with the help of an antenna. A transmitter is a radio sender. The set you listen to is a radio receiver. The radio programs you hear are sent out by transmitters from radio-broadcasting studios, or stations.

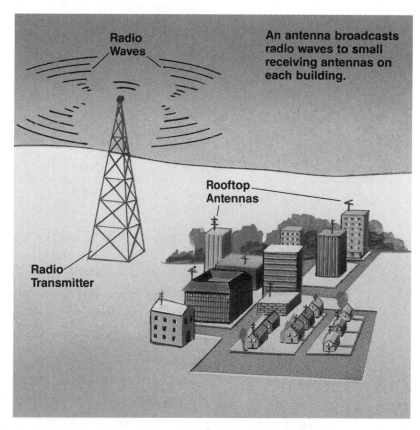

Radio Waves

An antenna broadcasts radio waves to small receiving antennas on each building.

Rooftop Antennas

Radio Transmitter

A transmitter makes an electric current that vibrates very fast. It vibrates many thousands or even millions of times a second. Such a quickly vibrating current can flow through a wire. When it reaches the antenna, however, it changes form. Out of the antenna comes an invisible electromagnetic field that extends for miles. Sometimes it even reaches halfway around the Earth. This field is made of radio waves. These waves can be picked up by a receiver.

What does an antenna look like?

An antenna can be a piece of wire, or it can be a whole mass of wires hanging like a net from tall towers. Some antennas are metal poles or rods sticking straight up. Others are dish-shaped. The type of antenna used depends on how fast the radio waves are vibrating and on how far and in which direction you want them to go.

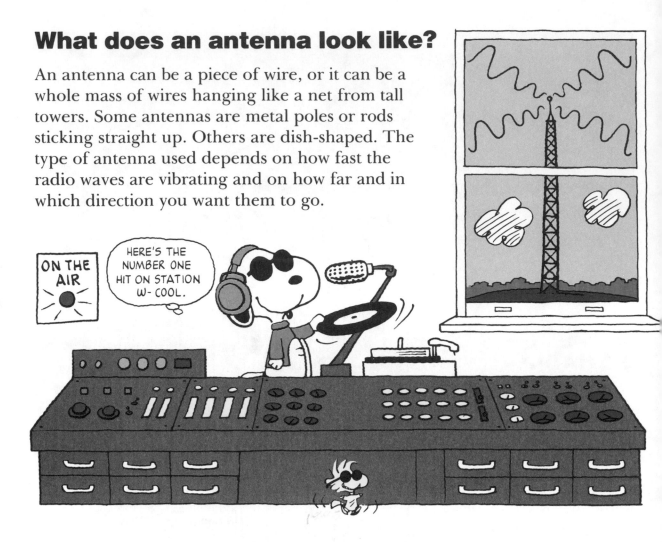

How do radio waves carry voices and music?

If you walked into a radio station, you would see someone talking into a microphone or playing music from a record, cassette, or compact disc. A microphone is much like the mouthpiece of a telephone. When you talk into it, sound waves cause a piece of metal in the microphone to vibrate. An electric current flows through the microphone. The current vibrates in time with the vibrations of voices or music. This current can travel only along wires, but the job of a radio station is to send this current out to radio receivers. The trick, then, is to get the microphone current to hitch a piggyback ride on the transmitter current. The combination can travel through the air or space as radio waves.

A radio transmitter has a part called a modulator (MOJ-uh-lay-tur). It mixes the microphone current with the transmitter current. In this way, the microphone vibrations can leave the antenna together with the transmitter's radio waves. That way the sounds travel through air as electric energy.

144

Radio waves travel in the atmosphere at about the same speed as light waves—186,000 miles per second!

Can radio waves be sent in a straight beam?

Yes. Most antennas send out radio waves in all directions. To send the waves in a straight line, you need a special antenna. This type of antenna is curved, like a dish. Radio waves come out in all directions from a rod pointing from the middle of the dish. Many of these waves then hit the curved part of the dish. The curve causes the waves to bounce back out, away from the dish. Then they travel in a straight beam.

A satellite dish can be used to receive radio signals from satellites orbiting the Earth.

Can a dish-shaped antenna receive radio waves?

Yes. Like most antennas, dish-shaped antennas can receive as well as send. Some, like radar antennas, send and receive at the same time. Dish antennas are very good for communicating with space satellites. They can be aimed directly at a satellite so that a clear, strong signal can be sent thousands of miles away. When receiving, a dish antenna picks up signals only from the direction in which it is aimed. The signal comes through very clearly.

How many radio-broadcasting stations are there?

The United States alone has about 9,000 radio-broadcasting stations.

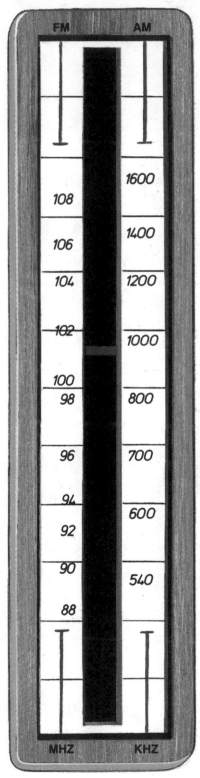

Why don't the radio waves from different stations get mixed up in the air?

When you play your radio, you turn the dial to a number. The number may be 700 or 1,000 or one of many other numbers. (There may be just a 7 or a 10 on your radio dial. If the radio is small, the zeroes will be left out.) Each number stands for a frequency (FREE-kwun-see). Each station broadcasts at a different frequency. The frequency is the rate of vibration of the waves that come from the station's transmitter. Your radio can "tune in" on the frequency you want to hear. Waves from other stations go by without being picked up.

TALKING TO FRIENDS WITH RADIOS

What is a two-way radio?

A two-way radio is one that can send out radio signals and also pick them up. The radio you have in your house is a one-way radio. It only receives radio waves. The radio transmitter in a broadcasting station is also a one-way radio. It sends out radio waves.

A two-way radio is the kind you sometimes see taxicab drivers using. They talk into it to tell the cab company where they are taking you. They also get messages from the cab company through this radio.

People use two-way radios in boats, airplanes and other places without telephones.

What is a radio ham?

In spite of the name, a radio ham has nothing to do with food! It is a person who sends and receives radio messages as a hobby. Many boys and girls become radio hams. They send messages to other hams by code or by voice. There are special frequencies set aside for them to use. In order to send messages, hams have to pass a test and get a license. They also must have special equipment—a transmitter, a receiver, and an antenna. Many hams build their own equipment from kits. If you want to become a ham, the equipment will cost anywhere from 50 dollars to thousands of dollars.

A ham radio operator can communicate with people in other countries.

What is a CB radio?

CB stands for Citizens Band. It is a group of frequencies reserved for ordinary people to use. You do not need a license to use a CB radio. Usually, people have CB radios in their cars. Truck drivers use CBs a lot. They talk with other drivers and find out about traffic conditions. A special language has grown up among CB users. It is a kind of code. For example, *smokey* means policeman. *Rolling double nickels* means driving at 55 miles an hour.

CHAPTER 19

Have you ever wondered how your television makes a picture, or how music comes out of your stereo? Well, if you have, step right up and take a seat. The show is about to begin, with the *Peanuts* gang helping you tune in with electricity!

LOOK AND LISTEN!

WATCHING TELEVISION

How does black-and-white television work?

The screen that you look at is the front end of something called a picture tube. The screen is coated on the inside with a chemical (phosphor) that glows when it is hit by electrons. The electrons come from a part of the TV called an electron gun, at the back of the picture tube. If you use a magnifying glass to look closely at the screen while the set is playing, you can see lots of thin lines running across it. The electron gun fires a row of electrons along each line. Some places on the line are hit by a lot of electrons, and they light up brightly. Other places are hit by fewer electrons. These places appear light gray, dark gray, or black. The darkness depends on how many electrons hit them. When you look at all the light and dark spots together, your eyes see a picture. It's like looking at a photograph in a newspaper. If you look at the photograph closely, you can see that it is made up of lots of tiny dots.

Screen

Antenna

The image on a television screen is made up of tiny dots.

How does a picture get to your television?

A picture gets to your TV in much the same way that sound reaches your radio. Radio waves carry the video picture and sound from a transmitting station, through the air, to your TV.

How is it possible to see color on a TV?

Color television is very much like a comic strip or a color photograph printed in a magazine. The picture is a mixture of thousands and thousands of little colored dots (red, green, and blue). If you look at a color television screen very closely, you can see the little dots. When the set is off, the dots look gray or silvery. When the set is on, the dots light up.

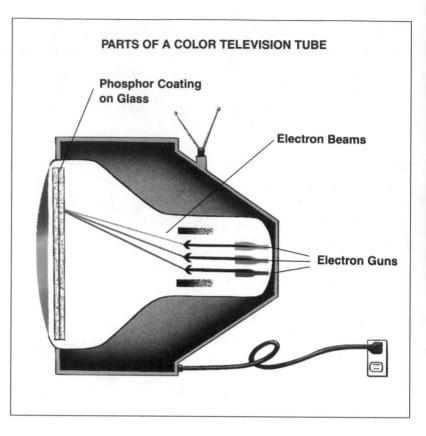

PARTS OF A COLOR TELEVISION TUBE

Phosphor Coating on Glass

Electron Beams

Electron Guns

The dots are made of a chemical (phosphor) that glows when hit by a beam of electrons shot from an electron gun. A black-and-white television set has only one electron gun. A color set has three, one for each color—red, green, and blue. Other colors—yellow, orange, purple, brown, black, and white—are made to appear on the screen by controlling how many red, green, and blue dots light up. For example, a picture of a glass of orange juice would be made up of a large number of red dots and a smaller number of green dots.

A color television camera separates everything it looks at into red, green, or blue. Then the television station transmits a red picture, a green picture, and a blue picture. The television catches these pictures with its antenna and sends the pictures to the three electron guns. The three pictures are mixed on the screen to show the same colors that the camera saw.

THIS PROGRAM WAS BROUGHT TO YOU AS A PUBLIC SERVICE..

CONSULT YOUR PAPER FOR A COMPLETE LISTING OF FUTURE PROGRAMS

AND NOW FOR A COMMUNITY REMINDER...

WAKE UP!

LISTENING TO MUSIC

What is a phonograph?

Phonograph is an old-fashioned record player or hi-fi. Today, most people use tape cassettes or compact disks (CDs) instead of records.

What is hi-fi?

Hi-fi is short for *high fidelity*. Fidelity refers to how accurately a record or stereo set makes sounds. A high-fidelity recording of an orchestra should sound almost exactly like a real orchestra.

What does *stereo* mean?

Stereo means a sound-recording system that uses two or more microphones for recording and two or more loudspeakers for listening. Systems that record with only one microphone and play back with only one speaker are called monaural (mon-OR-ul), or mono for short. That means "one ear."

The extra microphones and loudspeakers used in a stereo system make the sound more realistic. When you listen to music on stereo, different sounds come from different loudspeakers. For example, you might hear a saxophone on one speaker and a guitar on the other. It sounds as though the musicians are right in the same room with you. Listening to a monaural record is almost like listening to live music with only one ear.

IT SOUNDS ALMOST AS IF BEETHOVEN WERE RIGHT HERE IN THIS VERY ROOM!

YOUNG PEOPLE'S CONCERT

YOU MEAN, HE'S NOT?

LUDWIG'S GREATEST HITS

MOZART PIANO CONCERTO

151

How is sound recorded?

Sound is recorded in two ways, called analog and digital. With the analog system, the current from the microphone makes a needle vibrate so that it cuts a wavy line on a plastic disc. The digital system does the same thing, but the vibrations of the needle are controlled by a computer. The computer takes the microphone current and changes it into tiny segments that, in turn, make the needle vibrate. The digital system gives an engineer excellent control of the sound being made. That way, when the record is played back, the sound is very close to what it was when it was being made live.

How does a phonograph record make sounds?

The surface of the record is covered with tiny grooves that are close together in a spiral. Seen under a microscope, these grooves have a wavy pattern that contains information about the sound that was recorded. When you place the phonograph needle onto a record that's rotating on a turntable, the needles vibrate as it follows the "wiggles" in the groove. This needle has a magnetic field around it. As the needle moves across the field, it makes an electric current that varies. This current is changed to sound in the loudspeaker, just as the electric current in a telephone becomes sound in the phone's receiver.

A CD player uses a laser light to read compact discs.

What is a compact disc player?

A compact disc (CD) player is a musical device that plays compact discs instead of records. The first thing you notice about a compact disc is that it has no grooves as a phonograph record does. Rather, it is a very thin disc of plastic. No needles are used to play it. Instead, a tiny laser beam in the CD player below the disc reflects off the sound track to a light detector. This light detector then changes the light to electric current for the loudspeaker.

The sound is recorded on the disc by the digital method. A digital computer puts a series of tiny holes into the disc. These holes represent the actual computer code. When the code is played back on the CD player, the code tells the computer in the player which sounds to send to the loudspeaker. When the current gets to the loudspeaker, it is changed back to sound.

The compact disc is better than other recording systems for several reasons. No needle is used with it, so the disc is not worn out by the needle. Also, using computers, it is easier for recording companies to make changes in the kind and quality of the sounds that are recorded on a CD. In fact, the control is so great that a recording can be made without a microphone. The recording engineer merely types the desired code into the computer, and the computer directs the making of the "pits" on the plastic.

How does a loudspeaker work?

A loudspeaker reacts to the electric signal produced by an amplifier. Most loudspeakers have a moving coil inside a magnet. When the signal is fed from the amplifier to the coil, a magnetic field is produced, and the coil starts to vibrate. The movement of the coil causes movement of a thin, rigid cone that makes up the loudspeaker, and sounds are produced.

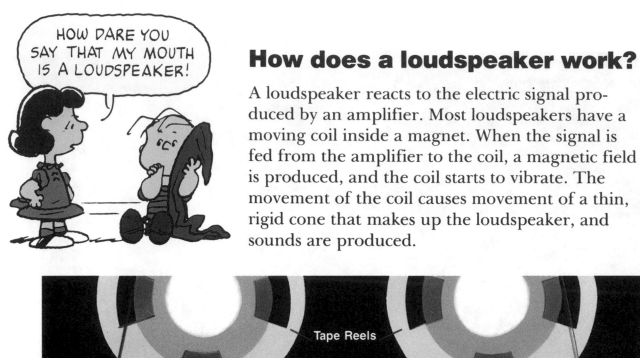

Tape Reels

Tape

Guide Roller

Pressure Pad

Drive Roller

Recording Head

Playback Head

REEL-TO-REEL TAPE PLAYER

How does a tape recorder work?

By magnetism. The tape is a plastic ribbon coated with a chemical—iron oxide or chromium (KROW-me-um) oxide. Each bit of the chemical is like a tiny magnet. Inside a tape recorder is an electromagnet called a recording head.

When you speak into a tape recorder's microphone, electric waves from the microphone go into the tape recorder. They cause vibrations in the field around the electromagnet. As the tape passes through the electromagnet's field, the bits of chemical on the tape are magnetized into different patterns. These patterns are a recording of the sound waves of your voice.

When you play back the tape, the patterns on it affect another electromagnet called a playback head. This electromagnet makes faint waves or signals that go into an amplifier. The amplifier makes the signals stronger. The strong signals make a loudspeaker vibrate. The sound vibrations that come from the speaker are just like the ones that went into the microphone.

Does a video recorder work like a tape recorder?

Yes. Video, or picture, recorders record both pictures and sound, but they work in very much the same way as tape recorders. A video recorder takes the video and audio, or sound, signals from the TV and saves them on a magnetic tape, which is similar to the tape used in a tape recorder. The videotape is larger than an audio tape because it must store information about the color and brightness of the picture, as well as the sound. The video information is stored on tracks along the tape—the same way that sound is stored.

Are there disc players for television?

Yes. There are video laser discs for movies and television. The laser disc is a digital device and can hold more information than a video-cassette tape, so the picture is more detailed and is better. The laser disc looks like a compact disc, but it is larger.

I'M A VIDEO STAR!

DID YOU KNOW...?

• Different appliances use different amounts of electricity. For instance, the energy used by a 100-watt light bulb in ten hours can keep an electric clock going for three months.

Alexander Graham Bell

• The fastest train on record is electric. It is a French train called the TGV. TGV stands for *très grande vitesse* (TRAY GRAHND vee-TESS). That means "very great speed." On February 26, 1981, the TGV hit an all-time high with a speed of 236 miles per hour.

IS ANYBODY THERE?

• The first words Alexander Graham Bell spoke into his new invention, the telephone, were "Mr. Watson. Come at once. I want you." He had spilled battery acid on his pants and needed his assistant's help quickly!

• According to legend, magnetism was first discovered by a Greek shepherd named Magnes. Shepherds carried wooden staffs with iron tips to help them climb hills when they were herding their flocks of sheep. Magnes noticed that sometimes the iron tip on his staff picked up pieces of black rock that stuck to the iron tip of the staff.

The black rock became known as magnetite. Before long, all the shepherds knew about the magic of magnetite, and they spread the news of this amazing discovery throughout the world.

• Early sailors used magnetite to make compasses. They found that the same end of the magnetite always pointed in the same direction—north. After that, the sailors did not need the Sun and stars to guide them. These sailors called their compasses lodestones. The word *lode* means "to lead," and that's just what the compasses did—they led the way!

There's much more to discover in Snoopy's World.
If you've enjoyed *How Things Work*,
you'll want to read...

People and Customs of the World

Earth, Water and Air

Land and Space

Creatures, Large and Small